The Original
Marvelettes
Motown's Mystery Girl Group

MARC TAYLOR

ALOIV PUBLISHING CO.
JAMAICA, NEW YORK

The Original Marvelettes: Motown's Mystery Girl Group
© 2004 by Marc Taylor

Book design by Sara Patton, Maui, Hawaii
Cover design by Lightbourne, LLC, © 2003
Inside cover writing by Susan Kendrick Writing
Manufactured in the United States

Publisher's Cataloging-in-Publication
(*Provided by Quality Books, Inc.*)

Taylor, Marc.
  The original Marvelettes: Motown's mystery girl
group / Marc Taylor
    p. cm.
  Includes bibliographical references (p.) and index.
  LCCN 2003113267
  ISBN 0965232859

  1. Marvelettes. 2. Women singers—United States—
Biography. 3. Girl groups (Musical groups)—United
States—Biography. 4. Soul music—United States—
History and criticism. 5. Popular music—United States
—1961-1970.   I. Title.

ML421.M398T39 2004   782.42'1644'092
                          QBI03-945

Contents

Acknowledgments

Marc Taylor would like to acknowledge:

First and foremost, I give thanks to God for selecting me as His vehicle to write this book, for providing me with the tools necessary to complete this project, and for allowing my life to be touched by everyone who was helpful throughout the process.

Thank you to my parents, Jacqueline Taylor Anderson and Donald Taylor. I thank God every day for you.

To George Anderson, thank you for being George Anderson, and thank you for everything.

Thank you to the original Marvelettes: Katherine Anderson Schaffner, Wyanetta Cowart Motley, Gladys Horton, Georgeanna Tillman Gordon, and Wanda Young Rogers, for your great gift of music.

Extra-special thanks to Katherine Anderson Schaffner for her dedication to this project, for her encouragement and understanding during the down times, and for sharing with me the most intimate details of her professional career.

Thank you to Gladys Horton for her role in initiating this project, for putting me in touch with her former singing partners, and for providing me with valuable information on the Marvelettes.

Thank you to the following people who granted me interviews. I am grateful to you for your time and consideration: Rosalind Ashford Holmes, Cholly Atkins, Annette Beard Helton, Robert (Scott Regen) Bernstein, Johnny Bristol, Delores "La La" Brooks, Larry Cotton, Wyanetta Cowart Motley, Louvain Demps, Georgia Dobbins Davis, Caldin Gill Street, Brenda Holloway, Steve Holsey, Ivy Jo Hunter, Betty Kelly, Beverly Lee, Dr. Romeo Phillips, Maxine Powell, Martha Reeves, Bobby Rogers, Robin Seymour, Shirley Sharpley, Kim Weston, Eddie Wills, BeBe Young.

Thank you to the following people for setting up interviews and for directly or indirectly enhancing the quality of this project: John Clemente, Glenn Dorsey, Pamela Drayton, Jeff Epstein, Ideal Entertainment, Susan Kendrick, Jacqui Malone, Sara Patton, Bob Swingle, Nancy Viola Taylor Thompson Walker, Don Thomas, Scott Westerman, Allison Wildman, Tom Williams, Sharon Young.

Again, thank you to Ray, Goodman and Brown—Al Goodman, Billy Brown, and the late Harry Ray—who gave me my first-ever interview when I was just "a kid out here with a pen and a sheet of paper."

Thank you to Billy Wilson at the Motown Alumni Association for putting me in touch with numerous people who were interviewed for this project.

Special thanks to Frank Johnson for his encouragement and guidance, for his *valuable* insight into Motown, the Marvelettes, and the girl group era, and for being as enthusiastic about this project as I was.

Special thanks to Frances Baugh for her role in initiating this project.

Thank you to Connie and Doris Sledge, Richard Wilkins, Gregory Thomas, Gloria Nixon, and Viola Marie Smith Taylor and family.

Katherine Schaffner would like to acknowledge:

Through one's life there are people who impact it. Many people don't have a clue what they may have done, and some just pass through.

To everyone who played a part in my life and in my career, I can't thank you enough.

God, who has watched my back since I was little, and still does.

Gladys Horton, Wanda Rogers, and Wyanetta Motley, THE ORIGINAL MARVELETTES, thanks for the time we've spent together, for if it weren't for you, this book would not have been possible.

Bob and Florence Anderson, my father and mother, who trusted my judgment and me, even if they didn't agree with it. My siblings, Sharon and Tim Anderson.

Keisha and Kalaine Schaffner, my daughters, I love you both. I don't know where I'd be if I didn't have both of you. I'm very proud of you.

Touré Schaffner, my grandson, my sugar bear, my running buddy, I love you so very much.

Uncle Frank, who let us practice on your tape recorder (Webcor) and hear all of our mistakes.

Pat Guest and Tracy Woloszyn, my best friends who listened to me moan and groan and heard me bitch and cry. Boy, do I love you girls.

There are many family members and friends I didn't mention. It's not that I forgot but (1) there are too many and (2) I would have forgotten someone and you'd be angry with me. Ha, Ha.

To our fans, I didn't know how much our music meant to so many people. I've met some of you and we've become friends. Thank you for your years of support and God bless you all.

Introduction

When the subject of Motown's golden era of the 1960s is broached, certain names immediately come to mind: the Supremes, the Temptations, the Miracles, the Four Tops, Marvin Gaye, Stevie Wonder, and Martha and the Vandellas. Rarely are the accomplishments of the Marvelettes, Motown's first successful girl group, discussed in the same context.

For this reason and others, *The Original Marvelettes: Motown's Mystery Girl Group* was written. The Marvelettes came to Motown Record Corporation in the spring of 1961; the label perhaps looking for a way to capitalize on the Shirelles taking "Will You Love Me Tomorrow" to the top of the charts. Before these five teenage girls from tiny Inkster, Michigan barely had enough time to blink, they gave Motown their first Number One pop record with "Please Mr. Postman." Other hits such as "Playboy" and "Beechwood 4-5789" soon followed, and the Marvelettes were one of the top recording and performing acts in the country. However, the group was unable to fully capitalize on its success. Motown was still an up-and-coming label with limited resources, and television exposure was virtually nonexistent. When Motown did become a powerhouse in the music industry, they focused on other acts. The girl group phenomenon had run its course, and the Marvelettes were no longer churning out hits on a consistent basis. Something was needed to give their sound more of an adult flavor. The group had a mini resurgence in the middle of the decade with sexier material penned by Smokey Robinson, most notably "Don't Mess with Bill," "The Hunter Gets Captured By the Game," and "My

Baby Must Be a Magician." Unfortunately, the Marvelettes could not sustain this momentum and, by the end of the decade, had disbanded.

The original lineup began as Gladys Horton, Wanda Young, Katherine Anderson, Georgeanna Tillman, and Wyanetta Cowart, gradually shifting over the years from a quintet to a quartet to a trio. Their earlier hits, aimed at the teenage market, featured Gladys singing lead, while their latter, more adult material had Wanda out front. From 1961 to 1969, the Marvelettes had over 20 singles to reach the *Billboard* pop chart, with 10 hitting the top-40. However, their accomplishments cannot be limited to vinyl. At a time when most girl groups merely swayed back and forth on stage, the Marvelettes had a stage act that set them apart from their female contemporaries, and they were generally regarded as Motown's most dynamic female act.

Unlike other books about Motown and its artists, *The Original Marvelettes: Motown's Mystery Girl Group* is neither an as-told-to autobiography nor an unauthorized biography. The story is told primarily from the point of view of Katherine Anderson Schaffner (affectionately known as "the tall one"), the only Marvelette who was there from the very beginning until the very end. She spoke of how the group adjusted to rising from obscurity to the top of the music charts in less than a year, the whirlwind lifestyle of a top recording and performing act, the Motortown Revue tours, the events surrounding the departure of her bandmates, how the Marvelettes were affected by the rise of the Supremes, their introduction to the dark side of the entertainment industry, and the group's breakup.

I tried to add some objectivity to the book by interviewing other artists and personnel inside and outside of Motown as something of a cross-check and a complement to Katherine's recollections. I also tried to refute certain erroneous information about the Marvelettes, such as them having once been known as the Marvels, and their mysterious member, Georgeanna Dobbins. Finally, since the breakup of the Marvelettes occurred with such little fanfare, and the original members never performed together in any capacity again, I wanted to provide readers with some information about what happened to them after 1970.

Everyone interviewed for the book was gracious, and nearly everyone expressed appreciation that a book was finally being written about the Marvelettes. I approached this project as something of a Motown historian, but with very limited knowledge about the career of the Marvelettes. However, hearing this story led me to conclude, "Wow, this is something that needs to be told."

If you are someone who fondly remembers the Marvelettes or happens to be a girl group or Motown fan in general, it is my hope that you will enjoy this book. Consider *The Original Marvelettes: Motown's Mystery Girl Group* to be your companion to the music of the girl group era and the golden age of Motown.

Marc Taylor
October 2003
e-mail: marc@touchofclassicsoul.com
www.touchofclassicsoul.com

CHAPTER 1

The Beginning

The city of Inkster, Michigan is located in central Wayne County, approximately 17 miles west of Detroit. As of the year 2000, the estimated population of Inkster was 30,115. The area was first settled in 1825 by Marenus Harrison and James Wightman. Another early and more important settler was Robert Inkster, for whom the area was named. Inkster was born March 27, 1828, in Lerwick, Shetland Islands, 50 miles off the coast of Norway. He was four years old when his father, a seaman, died; and in 1848, he and his mother took a ship to America. They ported in New York and spent some time in Ohio and Illinois before coming to Detroit. In 1853, Inkster received his citizenship from the court in Detroit and in 1855, bought a steam-powered sawmill with a contract to furnish fuel and ties for the Michigan Central Railroad. This mill was located on what became Inkster Road, just south of Michigan Avenue. In 1857, a post office was established close by the Inkster Red Sawmill and was given the name Moulin Rouge, which means red mill. Six years later Inkster was appointed postmaster, a position he held for two years, and the post office was renamed after him. In addition to operating a very prosperous sawmill, Inkster engaged heavily and widely in real estate, buying and selling property in Ohio, Illinois, Nebraska, and Montana. He also conducted business in the immediate area, as well as owning property in Detroit and Highland Park, selling his land in the latter region to Henry Ford. Inkster later moved to Kalamazoo, Michigan, where he died in 1914.

It is not known when the first African-Americans came to the area now known as Inkster. Some may have set foot in the region as early as 1688. However, many historians have put the year closer to 1701. The African-American's status in the area was probably that of a slave. Slaves in Detroit were used as dock laborers, carriage drivers, and personal and household servants. When the Northwest Ordinance of 1787 prohibiting slavery was passed, a limited number of Michigan citizens continued to hold slaves, despite the law. However, slavery vanished by the early 1800s. The Detroit region soon became an area where thousands of runaway slaves could find refuge. By the middle of the 19th century, Michigan, because of its accessibility to Canada, was the largest terminus point for slaves gaining freedom. Between 1840 and 1862, it is estimated that 30,000 slaves made their escape into Canada through Michigan. Some of the fugitives had to have passed through Inkster. However, African-Americans did not settle in Inkster until World War I.

The Ford Rouge Plant brought in an influx that found employment in the booming automotive industry. The population in Inkster grew from 150 in 1900 to 3,700 in 1920. By 1924, African-Americans began to migrate to Inkster in larger numbers. Encouraged by the $5 workday innovated by Henry Ford, and the proximity of Inkster to their jobs, southern African-Americans, through the help of John Dancy of the Urban League, found places to live in Inkster. By the time the area was incorporated as a village in 1927, African-Americans totaled 90 percent of the population. Inkster would officially become a city in 1964.

It has been argued that the transformation of Inkster from a village to a city can be traced to the early 1960s' achievements of five teenage residents of this obscure town: Katherine Anderson, Wyanetta Cowart, Gladys Horton, Georgeanna Tillman, and Wanda Young, better know as the Marvelettes, Motown Records' first successful girl group. Marvelettes founder Gladys Catherine Horton (alto-lead) was born May 30, 1945 (the original Memorial Day), in Gainesville, Florida, to parents of West Indies heritage. At nine months, she was given up for adoption. For much of her early life, she moved from foster home to foster home before settling with the Jones family on Harriet Street in Inkster. Gladys initially displayed musical talent by singing in the church's choir.

She recalls, "I got involved in singing with a church group called the Millenarian Specials. Ann Montgomery, who was one of the greatest singers in the world, brought me into the group. She liked the way I sang 'I've Been Working for Jesus a Long, Long Time.' That was my song, even though she sang it better than I did."

Gladys also enjoyed listening to popular music on the radio and sought out other girls who had a love of music and a passion for singing. At age 14, she joined with some friends — Jeanette McClaflin, Juanita McClaflin, and Rosemary Wells — to form a group called the Del-Rhythmetts. In 1959, this foursome recorded an obscure single, the Latin-flavored "Chic-a-Boom." The song was released on JVB Records, a small, independent label in Detroit run by Hastings Street record store owner Joe Von Battle. Outside of local airplay, nothing came of it and the Del-Rhythmetts soon disbanded.

"Rosemary did everything," recalls Gladys. "We recorded 'Chic-a-Boom' at Joe's Record Shop. Rosemary got in touch with Joe and set up the date. I was just a background singer, and I went along with it because everyone said it was such a good song. We got there, we recorded the song, they gave us a whole box of records, they played it once or twice on the radio, and that was that ... It was a good song. [Von Battle] got into singing himself later. He later heard about me being at Motown and that I recorded there.

"I don't think Motown ever knew about me doing that song. It's something that comes with your youth. If no one asks you anything, you just don't say it. No one asked me if I had recorded anything before, and I just forgot about it."

The short-lived career of the Del-Rhythmetts did not deter Gladys' musical aspirations. Upon entering Inkster High School in 1960, she immediately joined the school chorus, headed by Romeo Phillips. A native of Chicago, Romeo Eldridge Phillips was a trumpet player who earned Bachelor of Music and Master of

Music Degrees in Theory from the Chicago Musical College. He played for Eugene Wright (the bassist in Dave Brubek's quartet) in a local band called Eugene Wright and the Dukes of Swing. After a stint in the Army, Phillips relocated to Inkster where he would teach at the predominantly black high school from 1957 until 1966. He recalls, "When I got out of the Army, I was being hounded by the police. They just assumed that by me playing trumpet, I was involved in narcotics. The shakedown and corruption in Chicago was just awful. Two days after I was out of the Army I was accosted by two policemen and taken down to the 48th Street station. But it just so happened that when I walked in, the captain and the judge saw me. They both knew that I had been away for two years. After that encounter, I decided I would concentrate exclusively on [teaching] vocal and choral music."

Phillips was in charge of four music classes at Inkster High — a glee club, a chorus, a select group, and a male group. He often worked closely with Ed Aames, who was in charge of the band. Though numerous students came and went through Phillips' four classes, one who particularly caught his attention was Gladys. He notes, "The one who stood out was Gladys. A lot of kids were practicing for talent shows, and Gladys was by far the most talented. She also turned out to be a very good sight reader."

Dr. Romeo Phillips, Inkster High School music instructor, 1959. (Inkster High School Yearbook, 1959/Courtesy Shirley Sharpley)

"Mr. Romeo Phillips planted the seeds of harmony in all of his music students," says Gladys. "His patience is something I'll never forget. He worked hard at giving us the gift of music. We embarrassed him and ourselves at many of the school programs when the choir sang. After the performance, I would look at him to see his reaction, and there was always a quiet smile. I knew we could've done better, but he never scolded us. Under his direction, we learned how to harmonize and sight read, and many times I took lead in the choir songs."

CHAPTER 2

The Talent Show

One of the major events at Inkster High School was the annual talent show held in the spring. Gladys had begun attending these shows before she was enrolled at the school. When the announcement went out for the 1961 contest, she went to work auditioning members from the glee club to form a group. Gladys selected Katherine Anderson (second soprano), Wyanetta Cowart (bottom alto), and Georgeanna Tillman (first alto), each of whom was a year ahead of her in school and who lived approximately five blocks away. She recalls, "I heard on the loudspeaker about the talent show and said, 'Well, I'm going to get some girls.' I reacted immediately, not even having been a part of a group. I approached Georgeanna, and she brought Wyanetta and Katherine along. I didn't really know them too well ... I really didn't know George-anna too well, either. That same evening I had at least five girls over to my house for tryouts, and I chose [Georgeanna, Katherine, and Wyanetta]. All the girls I chose to be in my group came from Mr. Phillips' class because I knew harmony would not be a prob-lem for us. Katherine had a strong soprano voice, Georgeanna was the alto, Wyanetta could sing second or first on any scale, and I just kind of fit in wherever a voice was needed."

Katherine Elaine Anderson was born January 16, 1944, in Ann Arbor, Michigan (where her grandmother lived), and was raised in Inkster. The eldest of four children, she credits her paternal grandmother as the earliest foundation for her singing aspirations. She says, "My dad and his family all had very nice voices. My dad

Katherine Anderson, freshman year at Inkster High School, 1959. (Inkster High School Yearbook, 1959/Courtesy Shirley Sharpley)

had a beautiful baritone, and my uncle had a really nice bass. As I look back into much of my family history, it was more or less hereditary because my dad's mom did a lot of singing, and several members of her family were doing a lot of singing.

"My mother had hopes that one of her kids would be musical. I don't think she anticipated me being a singer. She was thinking in terms of playing piano. When I was younger, I also studied ballet. When I first started singing, it was in church where we had our little youth choir. Then we had our little choruses in school. I always sang in the little school choruses from elementary school all the way through."

Wyanetta Cowart was born January 8, 1944, in Rockport, Mississippi, and moved to Inkster at an early age. The eldest daughter in her family, she was initially influenced by gospel singer Mahalia Jackson and such jazz vocalists as Billie Holiday and Sarah Vaughan. Georgeanna Marie Tillman was born on February 5, 1944, in Inkster, into a family of girls and was named after her parents, George and Annabelle. Katherine, Wyanetta, and Georgeanna all grew up virtually within two blocks of each other.

Katherine recalls, "Georgeanna, Wyanetta, and I all lived in the same projects—the area where we lived, we considered it the projects. We all had our individual two-bedroom, three-bedroom homes, but it was still considered the projects. Georgeanna stayed like at an angle from where I stayed, but on the street in back of me, and Wyanetta stayed across the street from her. We used to all get together at each other's houses and play cards, and dance and listen to some of the music. My neighbors down the street used to listen to the more current kind of stuff because they were

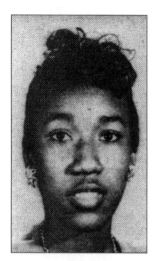

Wyanetta Cowart, freshman year at Inkster High School, 1959. (Inkster High School Yearbook, 1959/Courtesy Shirley Sharpley)

Georgeanna Tillman, freshman year at Inkster High School, 1959. (Inkster High School Yearbook, 1959/Courtesy Shirley Sharpley)

young adults by comparison to myself and my siblings. You heard a lot of the newer kind of music, and they were a really good, fun-loving family. On holidays, they played their music and their friends came over, who were older kids, so we always got all of the new music. That in itself became even more influential.

"Gladys originated the group because of the fact that when we were in high school, they were having a talent show. She was quite interested in the talent show thing and said to us, 'Maybe we can form a group,' because we all sang in the glee club together. I think Gladys' thing was, 'What else do we have to do? So let's do this.' We all went into it from the standpoint of having something to do. We rehearsed quite a bit and tried to perfect ourselves as best we could."

In addition to her three glee club classmates, Gladys recruited Georgia Marie Dobbins, a recent graduate of Inkster High. Georgia was born May 8, 1942, in Carthage, Arkansas. Her family settled in the projects of Willow Run, Michigan, four years later, after a series of homes was established there for World War II veterans (her father fought in the Philippines). She started singing at age five and was initially influenced by Ruth Brown, Etta James, and Sarah Vaughan. A childhood friend at this time was future singer/songwriter Nickolas Ashford, with whom she sang at Willow Run Baptist Church. As a teenager, Georgia began singing doo-wop and fronted several local groups in nearby Ypsilanti. In addition to being a vocalist, she was also a trombonist in the marching band.

Georgia Dobbins, junior year at Inkster High School, 1959.
(Inkster High School Yearbook, 1959 / Courtesy Shirley Sharpley)

She recalls, "I was the lead singer of a group called the Teen-toppers and then the Shamrocks. We had little green dresses that cost about two dollars. And we were full of ourselves. We just did little stuff, made our own dresses. We were just singing for fun. I used to sing up at some of the clubs in Ypsilanti. There were some little community centers where they had little parties and sock hops. They measured your waist to determine how many pennies you'd have to pay to get in. I was the lead singer. There was Barbara Willis, Rosalind Willis, Cecil Amerson, and myself, four of us. Our chaperone was [Barbara and Rosalind's] mother, Grace Willis."

When the projects were torn down in 1956, the Dobbins family was forced to relocate, and they settled in Inkster in 1957. Upon enrolling at Inkster High, Georgia entered the talent contests with various groups and always emerged victorious—a point noticed by Gladys.

"I already had in mind to ask Georgia Dobbins to be a part of my group," she says. "I knew she was the key to our success. She was not only smart, but she was very kind and sympathetic to us freshmen. She was also very attractive. All of the girls looked up to her, wanting to be just like her. She got along with the teachers, and she was always smiling. I admired her because she always kept us guessing what she would be doing on the next school talent show. She's the reason I used to go to all of the shows. She always came up with something different, and she always won. I wanted her to be in the group, so I saved a spot for her."

"I had previously seen Gladys at school," recalls Georgia. "If you could sing, everybody knew it. I was in music at school, so I knew everybody; but I didn't have time to be with anyone. I knew everybody and that was it. My mother was ill, so when I got out of school, I'd go home. I never did socialize.

"I had just graduated and [Gladys] needed another girl. She just came over to the house and asked me to sing background with her. I said, 'I already graduated. Do you think I can be in the group? The kids aren't going to go for that.' She said, 'No, you just come on, anyway.' She cleared it with the principal, and I started rehearsing with them. I just stood in and thought nothing about it. I had no thoughts that anybody was listening to us. We did it for fun."

As the girls began rehearsals for the contest, they started tossing around several names, trying to come up with a proper handle. They jokingly decided on the moniker Casinyets, a contraction of "can't sing yet," because they were still trying to perfect their craft. As the big day approached, Katherine recalls the nervousness. "I had never done anything like [enter a talent contest]; as probably Georgeanna, Wyanetta, and Gladys had never done anything like that either. At that point, it may have been one of the biggest highlights of our lives as teenagers. It was a lot of excitement because the big day was coming."

This particular contest was important because the prize for the top three winners would be an audition for Motown Records, Berry Gordy Jr.'s fledging label in Detroit 17 miles away, that had just scored a smash hit with "Shop Around" by the Miracles. In the contest, the girls performed "Fine, Fine Baby," an original tune written primarily by Georgia, that featured Katherine on lead. Unfortunately, they did not win, placing fourth behind a soloist named Millicent Morris, a vocalist named Clarence Finch, and a jazz band.

"I thought we did an excellent job," says Katherine, "but of course the popular vote was for more or less the popular people. As far as coming in fourth, we were all disappointed because we all knew the type of work we had put into it and to try to do our presentation of it. We were really rather disappointed because we felt that we had done a lot better than those who were chosen the winners."

Gladys adds, "A lot of things went on at that show. There was a guy who played piano at Inkster High School. We saw him and he said, 'I'll play piano behind you.' He had never rehearsed with us, and I felt that something wasn't going together—either the lyrics, the music, or the background—but I knew we were off. People said, 'Y'all sounded so good and y'all looked so good,' but with me having an ear for music even then, I knew something wasn't right."

Fortunately for the girls, their performance drew praise from members of the faculty, particularly school counselor Anita Cobb and student council advisor Shirley Sharpley. They were able to convince the school principal to let the Casinyets attend Motown's audition segment along with the winners. Mrs. Sharpley remembers the girls' performance. "I thought they should have won. When I complimented them and told them that they should have won, they asked me if I would take them for the audition down at Motown. I agreed because [their performance] overwhelmed me. They were really good. I forgot who our judges were but they were outside judges, and evidently

Shirley Sharpley, Inkster High School student council advisor, 1959.
(Inkster High School Yearbook, 1959/ Courtesy Shirley Sharpley)

they didn't have any musical talent or awareness. Some other people said the same thing, but most people abided by what the judges said.

"The kids had a telephone number and I followed through. I just called. It was Gladys who gave me the telephone number. I called and got an appointment."

A native of Detroit, Berry Gordy, Jr. (who is actually a "third," not a "junior") was born November 28, 1929, into a family whose hallmark had been ambition and family unity. However, Gordy's road to upward-mobility was not a smooth ride. He dropped out of high school at age 16 to become a professional boxer. Although he was a decent fighter, he gave up the sport after fifteen fights and decided to make his mark in the music industry. Gordy obtained his high school equivalency diploma and served an Army stint from 1951 to 1953 in Korea. After his discharge, he got married and began working in his father's plastering business.

At night, Gordy frequented Detroit's jazz clubs, befriending the vocalists and musicians. With a loan from his father, he opened up a jazz-oriented retail store, the 3-D Mart — House of Jazz. However, the neighborhood demand was for rhythm and blues, and the store went out of business in two years.

By 1956, Berry Gordy was divorced with two children, and he took a job on the Ford assembly line. During this time, Gordy began hanging out at the Flame Show Bar, a luxurious nightspot that was a showplace for top African-American entertainment in Detroit in the 1950s. It was also around this time that he became interested in songwriting. Through his sisters Anna and Gwen, who owned the photography and cigarette concession at the Flame, Gordy met several jazz artists who frequented the club and, more important, acquainted himself with Flame co-owner Al Green. Green invited him to write songs for the artists he managed, most notably Jackie Wilson, who had just landed a contract with Brunswick Records. With his songwriting collaborator, Billy Davis, Gordy wrote a string of hits for Wilson over the next couple of years, including "Reet Petite," "To Be Loved," "That Is Why (I Love You So)," "I'll Be Satisfied," and "Lonely Teardrops."

Gordy's songwriting success gave his sister Gwen and Billy Davis the impetus to form their own label, Anna Records (named after Anna Gordy). They secured a distribution deal with Chess Records, and the entire Gordy clan pitched in, looking for talent to sign. Berry himself first ventured into record producing via a secondhand record-making machine that he used to produce records for anyone who came in off the street and paid him $100.

In 1958, Gordy met fledging singer/songwriter Smokey Robinson through Jackie Wilson's new manager, Nat Tarnopol (Al Green had since passed away). Robinson and his group, the Matadors, were at Tarnopol's office for an audition. Although they failed to draw Tarnopol's interest, they did make an impression on Gordy, who chased them down after the audition to tell them so. He took the 18-year-old Robinson under his wing, and the Matadors soon became the Miracles. Gordy produced the group's first single, an answer to the Silhouettes' smash hit, "Get a Job," titled "Got a Job," and leased it to George Goldner's End Records in New York.

Despite a good run of hit records, Gordy had little money to show for his songwriting and producing efforts. He saw that it was the record labels distributing his music in New York City and Chicago that, so far, had profited from his talent. Prompted by Smokey Robinson's encouragement, Gordy saw that the way to make it in the music industry was to stop leasing records to others and begin marketing and merchandising the music himself. In January 1959, Gordy started his own record label, Tamla Records, with an $800 loan from his family's co-op called Ber-Berry.

The first song recorded on Tamla was Marv Johnson's "Come to Me" in January 1959. When the record became a local smash, Gordy placed it with United Artists Records for national distribution, just as he did with Johnson's subsequent hits, "You Got What It Takes" and "I Love the Way You Love." The Miracles' "Bad Girl" was issued on the brand new Motown logo in the fall of 1959. When the song broke nationally, Gordy sold the distribution rights to Chicago-based Chess Records.

To showcase his young artists, Gordy set up local revues, including two early 1959 shows at the Melody Theater in Inkster headlined by Johnson and featuring the Miracles, Mabel John, Eddie Holland, and the Rayber Voices, a studio vocal group that backed most of Motown's first acts on their early recordings.

"The Melody Theater was like a little, small neighborhood theater," says Katherine. "From where we lived, we had to cross over the track to get to the show. I saw Marv Johnson and Smokey and the Miracles there. That was the first time I saw them. It was on a Sunday, and if I wanted to go anywhere on a Sunday, I had to go to church first. That was mandatory or else you didn't go to the show."

In the spring of 1960, the Miracles' "Way Over There" was the first record released on Tamla without the Chess connection, and sold 60,000 copies, mostly in the Midwest, remarkable for an unknown Detroit label. That same season, Gordy got his first national hit when he and teenage receptionist/songwriter Janie Bradford wrote "Money (That's What I Want)" for Barrett Strong; a tune that shot up to number two on the R&B charts and made the top 30 on the pop charts. Tamla still was not equipped to break a national hit on its own, so "Money" was leased to Anna Records once it got hot locally. Near the end of 1960, Tamla scored its greatest success up to that point when the Miracles' "Shop Around" topped the R&B charts for eight weeks and crossed over to number two on the pop charts.

Gordy ran his company out of a house found by his second wife, Raynoma Liles, at 2648 West Grand Boulevard, sandwiched between a funeral home and a beauty parlor. He soon formed Jobete Music Publishing (named after his daughters: Joy, Betty, and Terry); the corporation Berry Gordy, Jr. Enterprises; Hitsville USA; Motown Record Corporation (a contraction of Motortown), and International Talent Management, Inc. (ITMI) to guide the careers of his singers. Soon members of the Gordy family were contributing. Berry's sister, Esther Gordy Edwards, gave up her other business interests to secure a vice-president post at Motown, where she was put in charge of developing ITMI. Her husband, state senator George Edwards, became Motown's first comptroller. Loucye Gordy Wakefield took a job as Motown's vice-president and was in charge of billing and collection. Berry's brother Robert became an engineer at Hitsville. A few years later, sisters Gwen and Anna were no longer able to make a profit with Anna Records, so the label went out of business and all of their acts were eventually turned over to Motown.

In April 1961, the girls and Mrs. Sharpley made the half-hour trek to Motown, suffering a flat tire en route. Although they were late for their audition, they were still accepted. Upon their arrival, they met Robert Bateman, the primary auditioner. Bateman originally sang bass in a vocal group, the Satintones, who enjoyed early local success on Motown with their recording of "Motor City" in late 1959 and "My Beloved" in early 1960. He also doubled as the Rayber Voices' bass singer and was partly responsible for bringing Mary Wells to Motown, having known her through a mutual girlfriend. Gordy encouraged Bateman to diversify his talents, and he soon became a chief engineer at the company's recording studio. Contrary to published reports that Bateman was the talent scout who brought the quartet to Motown, that distinction belongs to John O'Den, Berry Gordy's valet.

Georgia recalls how the girls initially did not make a positive impression at Motown. "They looked at us like we were little country girls. They looked at us like we were dumb. To them, we were little young, country, dumb-looking chicks. We were square. We weren't glamorous at all. We were country kids coming to the big city."

For their audition, the girls performed songs they had done for their talent show. Katherine was the first to sing lead, followed by Gladys and then Georgia. By the time Georgia stepped to the front, Berry Gordy was in attendance. Although everyone was impressed by the girls' performance, they were told they needed original material to record. "That was another disappointment," recalls Katherine. "Berry was the one who told us to come up with an original song. Our audition included songs that we had done for the talent show or had rehearsed for the talent show, which oddly and strangely enough, I was the lead singer. Where I got that brass from, I don't know. Berry said, 'The girls are good, but ...

do they have their original material? You can come back when you have your own original material.' You always get that 'but' in there."

When the girls returned from Motown, they agreed to meet at Georgeanna's house for their next rehearsal. Georgia arrived with an acquaintance, pianist William Garrett, who backed several of Inkster High's girl groups and who also had written a few songs. She began flipping through his briefcase of tunes and was drawn to one titled "Please Mr. Postman," a song that had only a few lyrics and no music. Georgia liked the title and wanted to change the tune from what Garrett initially intended to be a blues song into something more favorable for a young girl group. Garrett agreed, as long as he was given a songwriting credit along with Georgia. She recalls, "There was no tune to ['Please Mr. Postman'], just some writing on paper. He had no music to it at all. Neither of us really knew how the song went. We were green. I said, 'Alright. I'll just use your title.' "

Georgia, who had no previous songwriting experience, took the tune home and reconstructed it into a song whose lyrics pointed to a girl missing her boyfriend who has been far away for a long time. She is desperate to receive a letter or postcard from him and pleads with the mailman to recheck his bag for anything addressed to her. "I was standing by the window," she recalls. "I was waiting for the postman to bring me a letter from this guy who was in the Navy. That's how I came up with the lyrics. Then I made up the tune. I just hummed it over and over and changed it to the way it should be. I improvised."

"I thought it would be a month or two before Georgia finished the song," says Gladys, "but in just two or three days, she was at my front door singing it."

"We thought ['Please Mr. Postman'] was really a pretty cute song," adds Katherine. "We thought it was a very nice, cute song that would have been a young person's song or a teenage kind of song. It was different than anything that had ever been released because no artist had acknowledged a layperson. Georgeanna, Wyanetta, and myself had a very good postman, Mr. Johnson, who was very, very nice. We knew his kids and went to school with them. He was very friendly and would talk with us as he did his route. When you look at it now, the song is a salute to all of the millions of people who brave the weather, in any and all kinds of conditions in order to see that your package arrives to you in a timely fashion."

The girls returned to Motown a month after their initial audition and created a "buzz" at the company by having written their own song. "When we went to Motown with 'Please Mr. Postman,' they were excited because we had brought them original material. Here again, Motown was growing, it was building. So bringing in new material was like bringing in new blood. The few people who were there when we came, they were not necessarily of the magnitude you may expect them to be because you're a new company. You can't have everybody be perfect. You had a couple of writers, but you really didn't have a stable of writers. Therefore, it was vitally important to get original material. At that point, Robert Bateman was there, Brian [Holland] was there, Eddie Holland was there or coming into it. Robert had a little group, and Marv Johnson. When you have people that were in the business but not necessarily on the musical aspect of it at the time, then of course you're always going to be looking for something new and different."

It was also decided at this time that the group needed a new name. Opining that the girls were marvelous, Berry Gordy changed their moniker from the Casinyets to the more commercial sounding Marvelettes.

Before the recording of "Please Mr. Postman," Georgia was forced to step down. It has been widely reported that she voluntarily left because she did not want to spend too much time on the road promoting the record while her mother was at home with a bad back. However, this is only partially correct. Due to their ages, each girl needed a guardian to co-sign her contract, and Georgia's father refused to sign.

She remembers, "We were going through rehearsals for about a week or so before they brought out the contracts. When it came time for the contract, I presented it to my dad and he hit the roof.

He asked my mother, 'How long has this girl been singing?!' My dad did not know I could sing. My younger brothers and I were raised in the church and grew up a little strict. My mom would let me out. She knew I was having little rehearsals in the basement. I'm not knocking my parents but they thought that when they signed the contract, that if we didn't make it, they'd have to pay that money back. That was their understanding. They didn't know anything but going to work and going to church on Sunday morning. And by them being Christian, entertainment and night-club life was out of the question. That was unacceptable. Back then they'd call you 'fast,' 'no good,' 'won't amount to anything.'

"My mother's illness was also the reason why they wouldn't sign for me. I'm the oldest child in the family with six brothers and [my family] depended on me totally. My mother was ill all of my life.

"When my dad wouldn't sign my contract, it was just like somebody had snatched the rug from up under me. It's like wanting something and somebody just takes it away from you. You want to go, you've got your outfit ready, but Daddy says 'No.' That's the way it was for me. You've got your little dress and your shoes laid out and you're ready to go to the party but Daddy said, 'No, you ain't going.' I stayed in seclusion for about a year. I didn't even come outside. I was so hurt. I felt ... robbed. I wouldn't listen to the radio or anything. It wasn't until 1978 before I sang again.

"People in my [extended] family asked why I left the group and I told them my dad wouldn't sign my contract. A few of my relatives said, 'Why didn't you come and let me sign it? You're dad's square. He doesn't know what he's doing.' I said, 'Well, he's doing the best he can.' He worked two jobs. All he knew was Ford [Motor Company] and Shell [gas station]. But back then, whatever went on inside of the house stayed there. I was never a disobedient child."

When Georgia left, there was a matter of finding a new lead singer who could deliver "Please Mr. Postman" in the same manner for which Motown had contracted. Sensing that Gladys had the most commercial voice among the remaining four girls,

Georgia selected her to carry the lead. "Gladys had a lead voice and the rest of them didn't," she contends. "When my dad refused to sign for me, I got Gladys and told her, 'You've got to sing lead on this song.' "

The group's next step was to find a new fifth member. Their search immediately began and ended with Wanda Lafaye Young (first soprano). Wanda was born August 9, 1943, into a large Inkster family. Diminutive and strikingly beautiful, she briefly sang in

Wanda Young, sophomore year at Inkster High School, 1959.
(Inkster High School Yearbook, 1959 / Courtesy Shirley Sharpley)

the choir at Inkster High School, from where she had graduated in the spring of 1961, and was now contemplating a career in nursing. Katherine, Wyanetta, and Georgeanna knew Wanda, with the Young family living within two blocks of the trio. As Katherine points out, "We could walk from [Wyanetta's] house up to the corner and would be at Wanda's house." However, it was Gladys who sought out an initially reluctant Wanda to take Georgia's spot.

She recalls, "After Georgia wrote and taught me the words to 'Please Mr. Postman' and left the group, I searched for Wanda. Someone told me that she could sing. She was a terrific lead singer, and she had a strong high-pitched voice, which gave us more of a Chantels' sound. She was the greatest and fit right in with the group from the start. Nobody, and I do mean nobody, could ever wear Georgia Dobbins' shoes, but I couldn't have found a better replacement than Wanda."

The girls almost lost a second member at contract signing in Katherine, whose mother was apprehensive about her daughter going into the entertainment field. Katherine recalls, "My mother was very, very hesitant in regards to me being in show business.

In the Detroit area, it was a very new entity. With me being sixteen, she had to sign as my guardian. There were a lot of conversations around the kitchen table. My dad said, 'Sometimes opportunity only knocks once and this may be an opportunity that she may never have again. You know she's responsible. So why don't we let her go and do it.' In their discussing it further [privately], my mother did think about it, and she consented to let me do it."

In Motown's primitive years, artists were allowed to take their contracts home and seek outside legal advice. However, this was merely a token gesture on the part of the label. The entertainment industry was new to Detroit. Thus, there was no bevy of agents or managers positioning themselves to represent the artists on Motown's roster. The city was also devoid of any attorneys who specialized in entertainment law. In addition to Motown serving as the artists' label, ITMI served as personal management for the artists for 10 percent of their earnings. Few artists questioned this obvious conflict of interest. The city of Detroit did have other record companies, including JVB Records, Wes Higgins and Robert West's Flick, Contour, and LuPine labels, and Jack and Devora Brown's Fortune Records. However, none of these labels were as well known as Motown, particularly after the smash success of "Shop Around." If any aspiring artists found Motown's practices objectionable, there were no equal alternatives from which to choose. Nevertheless, the details of their initial contract meant little to the Marvelettes or any other Motown artists who were just grateful to have an opportunity to record for the company.

"For us, it was just the excitement of, 'We're going to do a record!'" says Katherine.

Michigan law only required that a parent or legal guardian sign contracts for anyone under 21, which was the case for each Marvelette. Many Motown artists were therefore accompanied to contract signings with only their parents, themselves foreign to entertainment law.

Katherine points out, "My mother did have a copy of the contract and she had gotten together with a couple of the other parents and did try to find an attorney that could help them in regards to the contract, but no one [in Inkster] was aware of entertainment and entertainment law. In Michigan, with [the entertainment industry] being so new to the area, there was no such thing as an entertainment lawyer. So, therefore, many of the attorneys, though good, were ignorant to the point of entertainment law. The only thing they could basically tell us was that we were contracted to them for x amount of time and x amount of this, that, and the other, and that, technically, the contract didn't necessarily benefit us as the artists, but it benefited the record company. There was nothing in the contract to protect us.

"Through the years when you're working, you don't necessarily pay attention to what is going on and what is transpiring in your business. You're called in to sign your contract; there may be an increase in it, there may not be an increase in it. As you get older, you realize what a big major conflict it was [having Motown serve as your record label and also as your manager], but it was a point in fact that there was no other [record] company in the area."

The eight-page document that each Marvelette received was Motown's standard, boilerplate agreement. There were numerous stipulations that any experienced entertainment attorney may have questioned: Motown would choose all of the songs the group would record, and the group would record each song until "the sides designated by us shall have been recorded to our [Motown's] satisfaction." However, Motown "shall not be obligated to release any recordings," meaning that just because a song was recorded, it would not necessarily be issued to the public.

The Marvelettes received a two percent royalty rate of 90 percent of the suggested retail price for each record sold in the United States, less all taxes and packaging costs. They received half of that amount for overseas sales. This was a group figure that had to be split five ways.

Per the terms of the contract, Motown was obligated to pay the costs of the arrangements, copying, accompaniment, and all other costs related to each recording session, whether the song was released or not. However, these expenses and others were to be recouped by Motown from the royalties generated by sales of the records that were released. This was a particularly troublesome practice for the Marvelettes as well as other artists at Motown who would record numerous songs that would not be issued.

If any of the girls were to leave the group, she would have no further right to use the group's name for any purpose. And Motown could replace any member of the group with any person the company chose, or could require the group to record and perform live without a new member.

This contract, which the Marvelettes signed on July 8, 1961, was to run for four years with Motown holding an option to renew the pact for an additional four-year period.

CHAPTER 3

Please Mr. Postman

Motown brought in Brian Holland and Robert Bateman to produce "Please Mr. Postman." Holland had met Berry Gordy through his older brother Eddie, backstage at the Graystone Ballroom when he was still a teenager. He had sung with some local groups, but under Gordy's guidance, began putting melodies to lyrics. He soon became part of a loose production team that included Bateman, Lamont Dozier, Freddie Gorman, and Mickey Stevenson. Holland and Bateman made some adjustments to "Please Mr. Postman" in order to fit it to Gladys' voice and also arranged the background vocals; thus, they took part in the writing credits. Gorman, who was actually a mail carrier, also offered a few suggestions and became one of five official writers of the song: William Garrett, Georgia Dobbins, Robert Bateman, Freddie Gorman, and Brian Holland.

Gladys, who was initially apprehensive about singing lead, found relief from Florence Ballard of the then-unknown Supremes who, along with group mate Mary Wilson, was at the recording session. During a break, Ballard helped Gladys with the ad-libs. Feeling more comfortable after a few outtakes, Gladys tore into "Please Mr. Postman" with a natural, down-home exuberance that would come to epitomize the flavor of the group's early tunes. The song was further enhanced by its high-spirited, adolescent background vocals and a thumping backbeat and tough drive production that featured 22-year-old fill-in drummer, Marvin Gaye. The end result yielded one of the great pop records of the era.

"After 'Please Mr. Postman' was recorded, I think it was a point of being on pins and needles," recalls Katherine. "You know that you recorded this record, you know that you recorded it for Motown; Motown being the record mecca for Detroit. You're anxiously waiting and not really knowing when your record is going to come out, because you have no concept of the time it takes to take it from the acetate to put it on vinyl and to mix it into a better song than what you originally recorded. You're just anxiously waiting, and I don't know that we actually knew the date of when it was going to be released. I think we just heard it on the radio."

"Please Mr. Postman" was issued August 21, 1961, and entered *Billboard's* Top 100 chart on September 4. A week later the song debuted on the R&B chart. "Please Mr. Postman" moved steadily up the R&B chart until it toppled Lee Dorsey's "Ya Ya" to reach Number One on November 13; a position it would hold for seven weeks. The song would also sit atop the *Cash Box* black contemporary singles chart for six weeks. However, on the pop listing, it did not make as smooth a climb. "Postman" inched up to 79 and fell to 81. It surged again, reaching number 30 and fell to 33. After some additional promotion, "Postman" jumped to number 19 and would crack the top 10 two weeks later. "Please Mr. Postman" reached the apex of the *Billboard* pop chart on December 11, 1961, 15 weeks after it entered the chart (taking longer to reach the Number One position than any record that had come before it), and gave Motown its first number one pop single. This was a remarkable feat for a black-owned recording company with black artists.

"We were all surprised when 'Postman' hit so big," relates Katherine. "The most surprised was Motown. But then again, hindsight is that there was a lot going on when 'Postman' was released. We were into, or going into the Vietnam War. We had a lot of young men that were leaving home for the first time going into the military, and, of course, some never returned. The timing of 'Postman' was excellent. When my brother went into the military, I know how anxious I or my mother or sister would be looking for a letter or something like that from him. One of us would anxiously be waiting to hear from him. [A letter] was the only means you had to find out how they were doing. Many of the younger men were out there on the front lines, so it's not like you could pick up the telephone and call them."

This chain of events happened at breakneck speed for the girls. In the early spring of 1961, Gladys, Georgeanna, Wyanetta, and Katherine had gotten together pretty much on a whim to enter a high school talent contest. Meanwhile, Wanda had recently graduated and was trying to find her professional direction. Yet by year's end, "without really trying," according to Katherine, the five girls had the number one pop and R&B record in the country. "Everything happened so fast," understates Gladys. "It was like one-two-three-four; the talent show, the recording of the record, the release date of the song, the date it hit the Number One spot on *Billboard*, all in the same year of 1961."

"Things did happen pretty fast," adds Katherine. "However, the other side of it is that it was very, very real as far as life was concerned, but it was a bit unreal because of your age. Because of your age you are extremely excited. It was pretty overwhelming that you were going to have the opportunity to meet Smokey Robinson and Berry Gordy. You're overwhelmed by all of these things when your 15, 16 years old. These are people, the Miracles in particular, you've heard about but never thought would be one of your peers. You are star struck."

Despite being at the top of the charts, the Marvelettes remained humble, perhaps unable to fully appreciate their feat because it came without years of struggle. Gladys recalls, "We just weren't big braggers. One day Diana Ross came to me and said, 'Hey, you've got the number one record in the country, and you're so humble. How can you remain that way? I'd be jumping all over the place and telling everybody I was this and I was that.' It was great that we had the number one record out and I should've been the one who was happy. I was in a foster home. I didn't know what I was going to do next, if it hadn't been for the record ... I just kept a level head and that's just one trait that the Marvelettes had; we've always been able to keep a level head about any and everything. We were just thankful and that was it."

The Marvelettes may have been grounded, however, they were also aware of being in over their heads, making a transition from everyday teenage life to suddenly having the number one record in the country. They knew they needed some guidance aside from what Motown provided and looked to their Inkster High School student council advisor, Mrs. Sharpley, for help. Unfortunately, due to family obligations, she could not make a commitment to the group. She recalls, "They wanted me to be their manager. I had a young child at that time who had cerebral palsy. So, as a result, I didn't want to be away from my family. I also had a son who was five years older than her. I knew [the Marvelettes] needed someone who was really behind them and for them, someone who was really interested in them other than for monetary reasons. I felt bad, but our home came first."

The success of "Please Mr. Postman" was a much-needed pleasant surprise for Motown. The company was just beginning to establish itself in the record industry and was determined to avoid the same fate as other black-owned labels before them that hadn't flourished. In Motown's formative years, independent distributors normally paid record companies for a current hit, only if they knew other smashes would be forthcoming. The distributors would otherwise keep the money from those labels who could only turn out a one-hit wonder. At the time, Motown had no new hits coming on the heels of "Shop Around" and many distributors withheld payment, which in turn caused Gordy to fall behind in payments to pressing plants and other suppliers. The million-selling success of "Please Mr. Postman" put the industry on notice that Motown would continue churning out hit records, and they were able to use this leverage against the notoriously slow paying distributors.

"When we had our first million-seller record, we were beginning to pump revenue into the company," says Katherine. "'Shop Around' was the Miracles' first million-seller, and it's been said numerous times that 'Shop Around' was [Motown's] first million-seller. However, 'Shop Around'—and it's been documented in trade magazines—was not. 'Please Mr. Postman' was the first million-seller record. 'Shop Around' had begun to drop on the charts, and it never did go to Number One [pop]. It dropped, and then after 'Please Mr. Postman' began to climb up, so did 'Shop Around.' Therefore Motown had the Marvelettes' 'Please Mr. Postman' and they had the Miracles' 'Shop Around,' and that's

The first photo of the five original Marvelettes, 1961.
(L–R) Wyanetta Cowart, Georgeanna Tillman, Gladys Horton,
Wanda Young, Katherine Anderson.
(Courtesy Frank Johnson)

what really helped keep the company afloat. When we had our record, Motown as a record company, thought it was going to take time to get to where they were going to be. But then they had five little black girls from the suburbs of Detroit that took them there a little bit faster than they were ready for. They weren't necessarily ready for that million-seller record."

The Marvelettes could only guess that a song that spent a week at the Number One spot on the pop charts and seven weeks atop the R&B charts was indeed a million-seller. Berry Gordy did not allow access to Motown's books to the Recording Industry Association of America (R.I.A.A.), which officially certifies million-sellers. With Motown still being an up-and-coming company, he did not want to pay the escalating fees the R.I.A.A. demanded, a fee that was based on the number of records sold. He also did not want the R.I.A.A.—or anyone else—to know how many records he sold. Motown would become notorious for publicly inflating record sales in order to boost the company's image and also the artists' morale. In each case, it worked. However, the label's artists were under the impression that they were selling more records than they actually were. When Motown presented an artist with their version of a "gold record," oftentimes it was just a Motown album spray-painted gold and framed. Yet, the Marvelettes did not even receive one of these "gold records" for "Please Mr. Postman."

Katherine states, "I really don't think Motown, Berry, or the writers at that time felt 'Please Mr. Postman' would do what it did. But I'm also a believer in fate and timing. How strange it is for five little black girls from a little town called Inkster, Michigan, to go to up-and-coming Motown—because it was beginning to get established—and come out with their first million-seller.

"My feeling about the whole thing is that to a point, the Miracles were there first and they should be the ones to receive the first gold record, not five girls from Inkster. But isn't it strange that we don't have a gold record? At the time, Motown wasn't registered with the R.I.A.A., and we can understand that because you are a new and upcoming company and to be a participant in those things costs money. But then, when you did become a member, why don't you reach back and get our gold record. Regardless of the fact of how the Miracles got their gold record for 'Shop Around' and anybody else that came around during that time, they still got gold records. Why didn't you reach back and give us ours? We have never received a gold record for any of our records that may have been gold, and they have been out long enough and have been re-released enough, that they are well over a million [in sales]. But then we never did receive it and we never have been acknowledged for our contributions to Motown, and I don't think that's an oversight."

Despite lack of proper recognition from Motown, having a smash hit record quickly made the Marvelettes the toast of Inkster, Michigan. "Many of the people who we went to school with, after a period of time, understood a lot better what we had done for the city itself," says Katherine. "Many people that did not live here knew nothing about Inkster. And by us performing and coming out of Inkster, then eventually they had to start putting Inkster on the map because it was just a small city. In fact, we were a little village and then we went into the city mode after the Marvelettes began to start performing all over the country. Then [the public] wanted to know where Inkster was. Behind everything, I think a lot of people were proud. They were proud of the fact that we were from Inkster, and proud of the fact that many of them knew us.

"There was a lot of excitement to it. I personally did not feel that I had changed, but I think many of my classmates very possibly felt that I had. I think it was more to the point that I was recognizable, that more people knew me than those that I just attended school with, or guys that I dated. When we started singing, there was some jealousy. You began to move away from those people because you didn't know who liked you and who didn't, and if they liked you, you didn't know why they liked you. There's only one girl who was my friend throughout. She stayed as a friend the whole time. It's like the rings on a tree to use a format. The inner rings are the people who you are close to and who you become friends with. You gain more friends as time goes on, but none of them can touch those who are in that inner circle.

"Being in show business allows you to meet people from all across the country. Therefore, you moved differently or indirectly, and not necessarily purposely, you begin to start moving in a different circle. You begin to start moving with people that are in the business because they understand it, and they understand what's going on with you."

The success of "Please Mr. Postman" brought on the inevitable demand for live performances; an often complicated situation because, with the exception of Wanda, all of the Marvelettes were still in school. There were occasions where Motown would have to give written excuses to get the girls out of class, such as for their appearance on *American Bandstand*. In addition, Gladys was an orphan, and thus, a ward of the court. As a result, Motown had to appoint a legal guardian for her. Esther Gordy Edwards' husband, George, was a Michigan state legislator. Through his contacts, Edwards was able to convince a probate court judge to let Gladys go out on the road, under assurances that she would be a chaperone and would make the girls study.

Katherine points out, "Mrs. Edwards is a businesswoman, and being a businesswoman she had that knack for being able to talk to people, almost like direct. There wasn't a very big staff at Motown when we came out. With her being at the company and us needing to come out on the road, she was more or less the chosen person to go out there with us, even though she was married and had a child. She's a helluva businesswoman. I'm sure that she was, in her own way, shrewd as far as taking care of business. Given those times, a lot of people, instead of acknowledging her for her business ability, would likely consider her a bitch because she had to be strong in a different number of ways."

Throughout these proceedings, Gladys had to write to the state of Florida for her birth certificate. She, at age 16, for the first time discovered her background. She recalls, "Mrs. Edwards and her husband became legal guardians for me. I was an orphan so early in life that it wasn't until I met her that I found out my real birth date, my middle name, my mother and father's names, and place of birth. I had to send off for my birth certificate for the courts to acknowledge and sign [the Edwards] on as my legal guardians over my business and money affairs. That knowledge opened up a brand new door for me. I discovered part of my roots and where I came from, the West Indies."

The Marvelettes were quickly added to a Motown package tour that was making stops in Washington, D.C., Baltimore, and New York. Katherine remembers, "Motown had set up a tour or a Motown Revue kind of thing and it started in Washington, D.C. We were not part of that particular package at the start of it. The Miracles, Marv Johnson, Eddie Holland, and Mary Wells were on that show. Our record was so strong with the people in D.C. that when [the other artists] performed, the audience chanted so loudly—according to what we were told—for the Marvelettes, that Berry had to call back to Detroit and say, 'Get the Marvelettes here. I don't care how you do it. Get the Marvelettes. If they can't come, get five girls, because people don't know who they are anyway, and have them out here.' That meant we had to leave school, get schoolwork, and almost do independent study. Contrary to what has been said through the years, we did have chaperones; however, we did not have tutors. That didn't come until much later in years with Motown. We were assigned a certain amount of homework, or work that we would do on the road, but time did not always allow for us to get that work done. When we came home, we turned in as much of it as we possibly could. You knew that there were any number of things that you could have done but you didn't have the time to do it.

"We did have time in between shows to do schoolwork, but it depended on the number of shows you had to do. If you were doing three to four shows, then you had time in between. However, if you're doing five or six shows, then all you would want to do when you got offstage would be to try to grab a meal or try to pull yourself together for your next performance.

"You had fun because when you had the opportunity, your pastime would end up being shopping. When you had some free time, then you would perhaps go shopping or when we first went to D.C., we did the scenic tour of all the different statues and monuments and things of that nature; things that you read about in books but thought, 'Yeah, they might exist but then again they may not.' We had the opportunity to go and view it and know that these different things do indeed exist. So it became an educational type of thing."

Motown needed to milk "Please Mr. Postman" as much as it could in order to generate some much-needed cash for the company. As a result, there was considerable pressure on the Marvelettes to juggle schoolwork along with live performances and other responsibilities that came with being full-time entertainers with a recent Number One record. However, as the professional demands on their time increased, they were pressured by Motown to drop out of high school.

Gladys points out, "Berry Gordy wanted the Marvelettes to quit school because we had a hot record out, people wanted to see us and at that time, Motown was able to sell more records when people could see us."

For Gladys, the idea of leaving high school early amounted to little more than something that came with the territory of having a hit record out. She further states, "The people of Inkster treated us really nice after 'Please Mr. Postman,' but later it got to where people expected you to wear diamonds and furs everyday. It was as if some of the people in Inkster were not ready for us to be ourselves after we had a hit record. They didn't realize that just because we had the number one song in the country we could come to school in blue jeans and ragged shoes. People felt that if you had a number one record out, you were supposed to be dressed up all the time, and we weren't. It became a problem two, three, four months after the song was out and students were talking about the clothes we were wearing. It really made school impossible. It was better to be at Motown, recording or watching someone record.

"When we went out on a tour with 'Please Mr. Postman' that covered D.C., the Apollo, and the Royal Theater in Baltimore, after going on the road and being onstage, school just wasn't interesting anymore."

For Katherine, Georgeanna, and Wyanetta, making a decision to drop out of school was a bit more painstaking because they were beginning their senior year during the run of "Please Mr. Postman," even going so far as to take graduation pictures. "Unfortunately, that was the choice we had," states Katherine. "Our choice was to [tour or] stay in school, go ahead and get our education. Wyanetta, Georgeanna, and myself would've been able to graduate with our class. However, after the Washington, D.C. people there and fans chanting for us the way they chanted for us, which to my under-standing was deafening, then we had a choice of staying in school or going out there and doing our record. I could not see, and I don't think any of the other girls could see us doing a record and Motown sending out a different set of girls than those that actually did it. We were the ones that actually recorded it so, why, if you were so family-oriented, would you think in terms of sending five [other] girls out there because the public doesn't know what they look like anyway? We had the choice of going out there or staying in school, and all of us ended up making the choice that we made the record, we made it popular, and we were going out there and representing ourselves.

"What Motown said about school, 'we want our people to graduate,' this, that, and the other … that's crap. They didn't really give a damn if you graduated or not. When they were talking about how there were tutors and all like that, that is not true. [Motown] never told us to finish high school. So if they say 'we wanted them to finish high school,' that's shit. It never crossed their minds about us finishing high school or anything else because we had a hit record and we were out there [on the road], so they really didn't give a damn. If we had come out with another record before 'Please Mr. Postman,' then it would've allowed us the time in order to finish school, but we didn't. Unlike the Supremes, as soon as we came out of the box we had a million selling record. Therefore, they didn't give a damn if we finished school or not."

Inkster High's music instructor, Dr. Phillips, remembers, "After 'Postman' hit, they began to miss classes; or if they did show up on Monday, they were just *dog* tired. Then sometimes they wouldn't make it at all until Wednesday. Of course, I had problems. I couldn't give credit for two students who weren't there. Then eventually they just dropped out ... That bothered me. That bothers me to this day.

"George Edwards, who was married to Berry Gordy's sister Esther, came to the school right after the girls, on their own, made 'Please Mr. Postman,' and he was encouraging them to drop out of school. In fact, I got on him because he did not stop by the office first. He just came into the building and walked straight back to the music room. He was talking to the girls, and they were expressing some ambivalence about dropping out of school. I think this was near the time they were about to graduate.

"My experience in show business, and also Mr. Aames' experience, conditioned us that one hit does not a career make, and I was raising hell with [Edwards]. We belonged to the same fraternity. He was saying, 'You have to strike while the iron's hot.' And I remember very vividly telling him, 'You can strike while the iron's hot, but unless the iron's plugged in, it's going to get cool.' I know they faced pressure from George Edwards and he went to the parents and the guardians of the girls and told them this is a chance of a lifetime, that they could always go back to school but they couldn't always have this chance. Once the record is out, they'll promote it ... The usual things that a promoter says."

"My mother was not pleased at all," says Katherine. "My mother is a very smart lady and her thing was, 'Well, they're dropping out of school. They're not going to get their education. She's not going to be able to go to college ...' However, my dad's thing was that sometimes opportunity knocks once and this may be an opportunity that I would never have again. After the two of them sat down and discussed it, the okay was given by both with their blessing."

"Ed Aames and I tried to get the girls to stay in school," continues Dr. Phillips. "We did not want the girls to be caught out there with no marketable skill. But then George Edwards went by their homes and talked about striking while the iron's hot. I will never forgive him for that—he's dead now. I'm *very* disappointed in him and I'm sure that fate would have taken a different turn for those young ladies had they stayed in school and graduated. That would've served as a platform for them to move onto something else *if* show business didn't pan out."

Katherine concurs. "Just a couple of years ago, about four or five, I went back and got my diploma. I graduated with honors and I did it through independent study. I've always found education to be vitally important. I was able to go back but, unfortunately, I didn't go back early enough in my life that I could've made something of my life after show business.

"The reason [Gladys] and I both are probably where we are in life right now is due to the lack of education. Some of the girls of other groups may have fared a lot better that we have, but for the majority of them, that's the reason why they are going back out there on the road trying to recapture what was, because we don't have the education to take us further."

As the Marvelettes became the number one girl group of the moment, Motown Record Corporation virtually became their life. There was constant rehearsing and recording as the company capitalized on the group's upward momentum. Gladys recalls, "Everything was work, work, work at Motown. The demand to come up with a hit was so great, Berry would tell us, 'We want *hit* songs.' That was drilled into our heads more than anything else during the meetings. Motown was like clockwork; everything was timed. If we had to be at the studio at four o'clock, the studio was ready for us. Whoever was in there from two to three or from three to four was out.

"Working with the original Marvelettes on any song was just great. Just being at Motown and working on those songs, even if you were in the background, was a great experience for all of us. We were just teenagers at the time. Motown was like our second home. No matter where you lived, you were at Motown every day, either recording or being down there with the other artists. It had that kind of feel to it. You knew you were going to be welcomed there, so you went there. Berry was there every day. He always said, 'If you need to talk to me, I'm in my office and I'm willing to talk to you.' That's the way it was in those days. That's [one of the reasons] why Motown was so successful. It had its doors open all of the time to the artists.

"Berry was mostly a meek, mild person. When he saw me, he would always ask, 'Are you happy?' It kind of made me feel good. By me being a foster child... I'd never seen my parents and never been around any family. For someone to really care enough about my happiness meant a lot to me."

As the primary lead singer of the Marvelettes, Gladys spent more time at Motown than the other group members. Rather than continue making numerous trips to Hitsville from Inkster, she would eventually move to Detroit, renting a room from guitarist Eddie Willis, one of Motown's early session musicians and also an occasional driver for the group. He remembers, "Gladys stayed with me until she went to L.A. She was kind of like my daughter, really. She was kind of a loner. She never did go out shopping with the other girls or anything like that. She was very calm and didn't really go for the boyfriend thing that much. She did have one, but it was never a big deal. She was going with Hubert Johnson of the Contours during the time she was staying with me. The only time she would go out was when he took her out or when she was going to [Motown]. If she wasn't going out with [Johnson], and that wasn't too often, she was just at home. Most of the time she stayed in her room. For her, it was about the Marvelettes doing their thing. When she was living with me, she was always at home reading a book in her room. That was her type of thing. Either that or she would be dealing with the songs, trying to learn them."

One week after "Please Mr. Postman" reached Number One on the *Billboard* R&B chart, the Marvelettes released an album of the same title. The girls are not pictured on the LP. Rather, a simple drawing of an empty mailbox with cobwebs is depicted, indicating how long it has been since any mail was delivered. This was a practice Motown used on all of its album covers in the company's early days. Berry Gordy was aware of the difficulty of selling black artists to white distributors and record buyers, and he was also concerned that record dealers, particularly in the South, either did not display records picturing black artists or placed them exclusively into black music sections. From the beginning, Motown did not want to limit sales to the black audience.

The Marvelettes were rare in being a girl group that sported two lead singers. In the early years of their career, it was supposedly difficult to distinguish between Gladys and Wanda. However, on a closer listen, the distinction was easily identifiable. Gladys was deeper and tougher, while Wanda was higher—particularly when she used her falsetto on some tunes—and more romantic. Also, as *Please Mr. Postman* was released less than a year after the Marvelettes had been singing together, it was evident how lacking the girls were on harmony. However, this worked to their advantage, particularly on "Please Mr. Postman," giving them a high school sound that hit the teen market at a time when the girl group phenomenon was beginning to flourish.

Please Mr. Postman opened with two songs led by Wanda: a cover of the Satintones' "Angel," a tune that sounded more New York pop than Detroit-flavored R&B/gospel; and "I Want a Guy," a song the Supremes also cut that year. "I Want a Guy" was virtually a solo effort by Wanda that had her character longing for a boyfriend who is different from the previous ones who broke her heart. He doesn't have to lavish her with material possessions. If he just treats her right, she will never let him go. Next up came "Please Mr. Postman," followed by its flip side ballad, "So Long Baby." The latter was "the ultimate goodbye song," says Katherine; a piano-driven track that was sung by Wanda in a novelty falsetto voice. Here, her character thought her guy would love her, but all he did was break her heart. Having had enough of his mistreatment, she tells him goodbye. "So Long Baby" credited Wanda's older brother, James Herschel Young, Jr., as the lyricist, who, according to Katherine, "dibbed and dabbed in writing." Just as with "Please Mr. Postman," producers Brian Holland and Robert Bateman made some adjustments to "So Long Baby" and took part of the writing credit. However, Young also got help on the song from Gladys, who never received a writing credit. She explains, "In those days, I didn't know I was supposed to get anything for 'So Long Baby.' I made up the music to the song, but you lose when you don't know, and I lost. It was my loss because I didn't know I was supposed to be on the credits. He didn't steal credit, nor was he overbearing or trying to talk me out of doing anything. I just didn't know."

Wanda and Gladys alternated leads on the album's remaining seven songs. The former fronted the tunes "I Know How It Feels" and "Whisper," while Gladys was out front on "Happy Days," "You Don't Want Me No More," "All the Love I Got," and covers of Barrett Strong's "Oh I Apologize" and the Miracles' "Way Over There." The contrast in quality between "Please Mr. Postman" and the album's remaining ten tunes is glaring and is a clear indication of how Motown had the Marvelettes hastily record ten filler tracks to package an album to capitalize on the smash success of one single. This is a trend that Motown would continue with most of its artists throughout the decade.

CHAPTER 4

Girl Group Phenomenon

The Marvelettes came to Motown at the beginning of the "girl group phenomenon," the first major popular music style associated primarily with women. Its origin begins in the 1950s in the music of groups like the Bobbettes, who were essentially a one-hit wonder, having their greatest success with "Mr. Lee" in 1957; and the Chantels, whose singles "Maybe," "Look in My Eyes," and "Well, I Told You" made them one of the first all-female vocal groups to maintain their success beyond one hit. However, these groups were rarities in a male-dominated field of vocal acts.

On January 30, 1961, the Shirelles (Beverly Lee, Doris Coley, Addie "Micki" Harris, and Shirley Owens), a quartet from Passiac, New Jersey, became the first all-female group to top the pop charts with "Will You Love Me Tomorrow," heralding the true start of the girl group era. The girl groups provided a voice for a generation of adolescents, in countless songs whose themes centered on romance, heartbreak, and the endless search for true love. The appealing honesty and sincerity of the genre was aided by the fact that the group members were primarily still in their teens themselves, and many of the songwriters of the era were not much older. Although the groups occasionally wrote their own material (such as the Marvelettes), it was their image that made them most identifiable with the female audiences that comprised most of the record-buying public at the time.

Given how the Marvelettes were Motown's only female unit to

have any success on a large scale during this period, and how their songs were aimed primarily at the teenage market, history has painted them as Motown's "quintessential girl group."

Numerous artists, including the Marvelettes, have pointed to the Shirelles as having opened the door for other girl groups. With both acts having Number One pop hits in 1961, the Marvelettes and Shirelles often shared the same bill, and the former have often cited the latter as something like "big sisters." Katherine points out, "The Shirelles and the Chantels, and all of the girl groups prior to us, made a major contribution in opening the

door for us and making it a lot more acceptable. We traveled with the Shirelles several times, and I became very good friends with Micki [Harris]. With them having been out there prior to us, they could educate us and school us from a woman's perspective."

Gladys adds, "The Shirelles were one of our favorite groups. I think they did a lot to bring the girl groups across because they were one of the first girl groups to have hits. We watched them onstage, such as the way they took their bows. They were just great and even though they knew they were great, they didn't flaunt their greatness and they weren't big braggers. They opened the door for many girl groups because they were great."

"The Marvelettes were bubbly, sweet young ladies," says Beverly Lee

THE SHIRE

The Shirelles had a Number One hit with "Will You Love Me Tomorrow" in January 1961, and opened the door for other girl groups. (clockwise from top) Micki Harris, Shirley Owens, Beverly Lee, Doris Coley.
(author's collection)

of the Shirelles. "They were wonderful. We took a liking to them instantly; all of them. They were wonderful ladies, and their stage act was great, very refreshing. They reminded me of us a little. They were full of energy and had powerful moves. They were just bursting with energy. It was very exciting, and they brought a new approach to performing."

She adds, "For so many years, it was a male-dominated field. It was refreshing when some women came along. It was like, 'let's see what they can do.' People had the perception that there was a lot of cat-fighting going on with the girl groups, but that wasn't true. Every show was like a family reunion. We would go from the Apollo to the Uptown to the Royal to the Howard, and each time you would leave messages for the next group. You always knew who was coming the following week. We would leave notes in the dressing rooms, or with the stagehands, or sometimes we would just leave a message on the wall."

The girl group era has often been overlooked by music historians who tend to regard the female acts as interchangeable, or worse, disposable, while the ones with the "real" talent were the behind-the-scenes players of songwriters and producers. Also, due to the short life expectancy of many of the groups and the influx of successors, the role of the "girl" in girl groups has greatly been diminished. Like the disco era some 15 years later, the persistent stereotype has been the assumption that any group of girls with the ability to carry a tune could have a hit as long as they followed the direction of the male producers who were calling the shots.

Unfortunately for the groups, their dependence on their manager/songwriting/production teams around them did put them at a disadvantage as far as maintaining their careers after the initial flush of success. Once a winning formula for a group had been identified, it was repeated in subsequent singles until the group stopped having hits. The act was then left to wallow in obscurity while the production teams moved on to the next formula and the next group. Because of their age and lack of knowledge about the music industry, the groups were unsure how to go about voicing their concerns, leaving them at a disadvantage. Rarely, if ever, did the groups have any involvement, let alone control, in any decisions affecting their careers. With the focus on getting hits being the primary goal, it was easy to overlook the feelings of the group members, particularly since they were considered the most expendable part of the equation.

The Marvelettes experienced not having any involvement in decisions affecting their career upon the release of their follow-up single, "Twistin' Postman," issued a week before "Please Mr. Postman" topped the pop charts. "Twistin' Postman" started off with a slow 13-second intro before changing tempo to a brisk beat, featuring handclaps and crash cymbals anchored by a frantic piano. The song, written and produced by Robert Bateman, Brian Holland, and Mickey Stevenson, employed virtually the same theme as its predecessor. Here, Gladys' character is about to give up on her boyfriend until she receives the letter from him, for which she had originally waited. For this single, Motown obviously sought to exploit the popularity of the new dance craze, "The Twist," of which Chubby Checker's single of the same name had topped the pop chart in the fall of 1960 and would repeat that feat for two weeks at the beginning of 1962. Unfortunately for the Marvelettes, the ploy did not work as "Twistin' Postman" was too inferior to its predecessor to be a big hit. The song reached number 13 on the *Billboard* R&B chart in early 1962 and peaked at number 34 on the pop chart.

Katherine points out, "You eventually learned that there were ups and downs in the business, and to be able to follow any number one record with another number one record, you would've had to have been a well-established organization. After 'Please Mr. Postman,' Motown was trying to jump onto the 'Twist' bandwagon, so the next record they dropped on us was 'Twistin' Postman' ... Well, it was only going to be but so big. We really didn't perform it that much. ['Twistin' Postman'] was one of the songs that we could've very well done without. I didn't see any reason to record it, but who am I? I'm just a peon. Of course, we didn't have any say-so in what was and was not released."

Motown would quickly learn from their mistake made with the

Marvelettes and develop a successful strategy to capitalize on the smash success of a previous single. Going forward, Motown would change the title and the storyline, keeping only the same arrangement as its predecessor. This was epitomized when Martha and the Vandellas followed "(Love is Like a) Heat Wave" with "Quicksand" in the fall of 1963, and when the Four Tops followed "I Can't Help Myself" with "It's the Same Old Song" in the summer of 1965.

During the run of "Twistin' Postman," the Marvelettes' initial hit remained in the spotlight when Philadelphia's Dee Dee Sharp reached Number One on the *Billboard* R&B chart and number two on its pop chart in the spring of 1962 with "Mashed Potato Time," a song similar in melody to "Please Mr. Postman." Motown sued Cameo Records for copyright infringement. With a girl group and a female solo artist at or near the top of the charts at the same time, it was inevitable that the Marvelettes and Sharp would appear on the same show. Nevertheless, the artists did not allow a potentially awkward situation to create a rift. Gladys explains, "Even though Dee Dee Sharp had copied 'Mashed Potato Time' off of 'Please Mr. Postman,' we were friends. Dee Dee's attitude was one that a lot of us didn't like at the time because she was into 'starring the show' and she was into 'Miss Dee Dee Sharp.' We were doing a boat tour in Boston, and she said, 'I'm starring the show and I'm doing six songs, so you girls are coming on before me and you do four songs.' We said, 'Okay.' Come to find out that the Marvelettes were supposed to be starring the show and Dee Dee told our chaperone, 'Oh, they don't want that spot on the show. We've already talked about it. They're going to come on first and I'm going to come on second.' Our chaperone, Mrs. Johnson, said, 'The Marvelettes are perfectly satisfied with their [headliner] position on the show.' It just goes to show that the Marvelettes were country girls. We just didn't have that city-like attitude that Dee Dee Sharp had. I felt her 'Mashed Potato Time' was a lot like 'Postman,' but the story line was so different. It was about doing a dance, so I didn't take it any kind of way and I didn't feel anything about it. At the time everybody wanted to get a hit record, and everybody wanted to be on the show with each other. We were lovey-dovey girls and that was that. The company sued, they had a big lawsuit, but as far as the artists, the Marvelettes and Dee Dee Sharp have always been friends."

Today the five writers of "Please Mr. Postman" — William Garrett, Georgia Dobbins, Robert Bateman, Freddie Gorman, and Brian Holland — are credited by the performing rights organization BMI as the songwriters of "Mashed Potato Time" instead of the tune's original composers, Harry Land and Jon Sheldon.

To capitalize on "Twistin' Postman," the Marvelettes released an album in April 1962, entitled *Smash Hits of 1962*. When 1962 became 1963, the album was re-titled *The Marveletts* (spelled incorrectly on the front of the LP) *Sing*. Again, the girls were not pictured on the cover. The album was produced by Mickey Stevenson and consisted primarily of cover versions of recent hits. The LP opened with a remake of Dee Dee Sharp's "Mashed Potato Time." Perhaps this was a ploy for Motown to bolster its claim that the original version was a "Please Mr. Postman" rip-off. The arrangement of "Mashed Potato Time" was eerily similar to "Please Mr. Postman," particularly with the background vocals, and it appeared that Gladys was simply singing a different set of lyrics over the same "Postman" production. Next up came the sparsely produced "Love Letters," originally a pop hit for Dick Haymes in 1945 (the title song from the movie starring Jennifer Jones), and more recently a number two R&B hit for Ketty Lester in the spring of 1962. This was followed by a remake of Mary Wells' hit "The One Who Really Loves You." On this tune, Stevenson simply lifted Wells' voice from the original music track and used Gladys' vocal instead. Gladys also sang lead on Sam Cooke's "Twistin' the Night Away." Wanda took over lead vocals on the next track, a cover of Bruce Channel's 1962 number one pop hit "Hey! Baby." After "Twistin' Postman" followed in sequence, Wanda again sang lead on a cover of Elvis Presley's "Good Luck Charm." Stevenson lent vocal support behind Gladys' lead on "Slow Twist," a remake of Chubby Checker and Dee Dee Sharp's "Slow Twistin'." Wanda returned to the lead for the album's final two songs: a cover of Clyde McPhatter's 1962 pop hit "Lover Please" and Roy Orbison's

"Dream Baby." Perhaps, due to its lack of originality, *Smash Hits of 1962* is generally regarded as the group's least flattering album.

Unbeknownst to the other Marvelettes, Wanda was pregnant with her first child when she was asked to join the group. During the course of "Twistin' Postman," she was forced to drop out for a time. "I did not know Wanda was pregnant," claims Gladys. "I knew she was studying to be a nurse and she told me she always wanted to sing. She turned down her nursing career to sing, so she saw a longer career in music than in nursing. I think what it was, was that she knew she was pregnant and would need some money right away."

The group in early 1962, minus Wanda, who was on maternity leave. (clockwise from top right) Gladys, Wyanetta, Katherine, Georgeanna.
(author's collection)

The group's road manager, Joe Schaffner, had been dating Florence Ballard of the Supremes and suggested that she join the Marvelettes to complete dates on an upcoming tour. Contracts with promoters called for there to be five Marvelettes onstage. Since the Supremes were still sitting on the sidelines at Motown with virtually nothing to do, Schaffner recruited Ballard as a temporary Marvelette.

"We were a bit disappointed [about Wanda's pregnancy]," says Katherine, "because it was like … let's get the show on the road. Since we had to go on out there, we would've preferred for an original group to go out there, but instead Florence went out there with us to take Wanda's spot. Florence had a helluva voice, and she had very good range. With Wanda pretty much singing soprano, Florence more or less easily fit into the group because not too many people had seen Wanda. A lot of the places in part where we were performing, some of them were new, some of them were old, but your contract called for five [girls], and there was no way [club promoters] would be that flexible. They wanted five to appear. Motown did ask them to reconsider in regards to that fact but most promoters would not do it because we were known for having five. Wanda was barely a good five feet but [most of the public] hadn't seen her. Florence had the height to fit in. With myself being about 5' 7", Florence would be approximately the same height as myself, which would've helped to balance [our appearance]. Even though Wyanetta wasn't out there all that long, she was tall. On top of that, there weren't too many girls at Motown that could've filled the slot. The Supremes were pretty much the only girl group that was there."

Although Ballard's voice, height, and availability made her the logical choice to become a temporary Marvelette, it was not a completely smooth ride. The Marvelettes were a high-energy stage act with an emphasis on choreography, and Ballard was not a particularly gifted dancer. Katherine recalls, "Florence wasn't much of a dancer. She found the choreography rather hard because we were a group with a lot of movement; we were quite active. There are some people who are dancers and there are some people who are not. She fell in the category of middle-of-the-road; she wasn't really a dancer, per se."

During Ballard's time with the Marvelettes, she roomed with Gladys, with whom she quickly formed a bond. Having discovered a common ground in traumatic childhood/teenage experiences, Ballard shared with Gladys her harrowing experience of being raped as a teenager, something no one at Motown outside of Ballard's fellow Supremes, Diana Ross and Mary Wilson, knew about. Gladys recalls, "Florence was really quiet. She came with us to learn about traveling on the road with a known group. It was at that time she told me about her rape. I was discussing with her that I had been brought up in a foster home. We were discussing bad times, and that's when she told me about it. Sometimes when you're young, things don't touch you as bad, and I looked at it as a part of her growing up. This was something that she went through, which was bad. Living in a foster home was sometimes bad.

"Florence and I roomed together but I didn't learn a lot about her. We were working a lot with Gladys Knight and the Pips and she had fallen for William [Guest]. We used to talk about him a lot. She would ask, 'Was he looking at me?' and I would say 'Yeah, he was looking at you.'"

Ballard's tenure as a Marvelette merely lasted one tour. Wanda had a strong enough support system—her mother, sisters, and daughter's father—to juggle being a parent and an entertainer."

The Marvelettes bounced back in the spring of 1962 with "Playboy." Gladys sang lead on this track in which her character tells other girls to look out for a Casanova. However, she alternates between warning the girls and singing to the actual ladies' man, telling him to keep his distance from her because of the other girls whose hearts he broke before. Brian Holland and Robert Bateman handled the song's sparse production: a piano-driven track backed with a subtle drumbeat, featuring handclaps at the beginning and at the end. Upon its release on April 9, 1962, "Playboy" would reach number seven on the *Billboard* pop chart and number three on its R&B chart. It accomplished a similar feat on the *Cash Box* chart: climbing to number eight on the pop side and number two for a week on its black contemporary singles chart. "Playboy" also reached number three on WABC's prestigious New York top song survey. Gladys wrote "Playboy," yet as with "Please Mr. Postman," Holland and Bateman added their finishing touches and received writing credits. However, in the somewhat generous or perhaps dubious climate of songwriting, Mickey Stevenson received a full songwriting credit for "Playboy" amid accusations that his writing contribution to the song was minimal.

Gladys explains, " 'Playboy' was a song that I wrote, and I wrote it by myself. I was just trying to copy off of Georgia Dobbins with 'Please Mr. Postman' but it didn't come out as good. It was one of those songs that Mickey Stevenson, Brian Holland and Robert Bateman's names are on, but their names should not have been

A rare photo of Florence Ballard with the Marvelettes (center
and bottom) during a performance at the Apollo, March 1962.
(L–R) Florence, Katherine, Wyanetta, Georgeanna.
Gladys is in the upper right hand corner.
(Katherine Schaffner Collection)

on it. I wrote that song by myself. Now that I'm in my fifties, I realize that when you write a song, if you're the only one there at the time the song is being written, your name is supposed to be the only one on the front cover. There's a songwriter's income that you can negotiate with other writers, but whenever you put their names on the cover, that gives them the right to divide the royalties evenly. That's what a songwriter lawyer told me and that's what happened with 'Playboy.' Mickey Stevenson['s writing contribution] came in on the end with [one line]. He told me his name is supposed to be on the writing of it, I believed him, and his name went down. If he did that same thing today, the answer would be, 'Ohhh, no,' but you live and you learn."

Two of the biggest hits the Marvelettes would have, "Please Mr. Postman" and "Playboy," were written primarily by group members; a rarity among girl groups in the 1960s. Yet Motown chose not to cultivate any writing talent the girls had. As the company was growing, it attracted talented writers; thus, they were less dependent on its artists assuming the role of writer. On occasion, Marvin Gaye, and later Stevie Wonder, would write their own songs and, of course, Smokey Robinson wrote for the Miracles and virtually every other act on Motown's roster. Yet when it came to its female artists, the prevailing attitude was "singers are singers, and writers are writers." Katherine points out, "Motown didn't let you write a whole lot. We didn't write too many things because [Motown's stable of writers and producers] more or less had a lock on that. They wouldn't let artists write, or if they did, they took a big cut of it. With Gladys, they took a big cut of her stuff."

The Motown rumor mill has also pointed to something of an unwritten rule that if an artist wrote a song, he had to give a producer part of it in order to get it recorded. Former Motown artist Kim Weston, who recorded such hits as "It Takes Two" (a duet with Marvin Gaye) and "Take Me in Your Arms (Rock Me a Little While)," was married to the A&R chief and producer, Mickey Stevenson. She claims, "There were some cases ... Motown was a closed situation where you could not get in unless you knew somebody. And if you knew somebody, I think it's only right that you compensate the person that helps you get in a major situation like that. That's how it was."

Brenda Holloway was a West Coast–based Motown artist in the 1960s, who scored a major hit in 1964 with "Every Little Bit Hurts." She was also one of the few Motown female artists who wrote songs; her "You've Made Me So Very Happy" was a huge hit for Blood, Sweat and Tears in 1969, and her song "Ba Ba Ba" ended up on the Supremes' *Reflections* album. She points out, "If you wanted your song out, you better [share songwriting credits]. If I'm a homeowner and you want to get something from me, you have to go through me to get it. You have to go through my terms … I'm the one who doesn't have it, you're the one who has it. It's no more than fair. I've made money off of 'You've Made Me So Very Happy' for over thirty years. I'm making more money now than I did in the '60s and '70s. That's where your money is, in writing. You're going to have to always give up something to get something. You have to understand business, big business, recording business. You can always have a complaint, always have a problem, but you need to work on a solution. You have to look at it as a business investment. If I had fought with Berry and told him I'm not giving anything up, 'You've Made Me So Very Happy' wouldn't have made me [a mid five-figure income] last year. You've got to give something up. You've got to be a business-woman."

With the Marvelettes riding high, there was continuous pressure on them as one of Motown's top artists at a time when the label was still growing and needed the girls to pump revenue into the company. As a result, they were constantly touring. As the Marvelettes were the girl group that Motown experimented with on the road, the girls endured less that desirable accommodations, food, and travel. This proved to be too much for Wyanetta, who suffered a nervous breakdown. Apparently never completely comfortable before the spotlight, she inadvertently made reference on Dick Clark's *American Bandstand* that the girls were from Detroit, a suburb of Inkster; a remark that made her the butt of much teasing from others at Motown. Wyanetta ended her career as a performer in the late spring of 1962, although she did continue to record as a Marvelette until the beginning of 1963.

Katherine recalls, "To lose Wyanetta was really scary. It was scary because of what transpired. I began to see very early in the game that the pressure was beginning to get to Wyanetta, and oftentimes she and I would be around each other quite a lot. I began to see it very early. In the beginning stages, our primary mode of travel was by van and after a period of time, we were in a Pontiac station wagon. We didn't necessarily get the opportunity to eat right; we didn't get the necessary sleep that was needed. The stress and strain of the whole ordeal was quite exhausting. So after a period of time, I just imagine the wear and tear of all of that and the change of today you're here, tomorrow you're somewhere else, you begin to almost lose where you are. And sometimes these things play really, really hard on you. When we were on the road, our mode of travel was always driving and you're sleeping in these cars. I would think that maybe what happened was it was entirely too much and it was entirely too hard. Gradually, as time went on, I don't recall that she ever said anything about it. She may have been feeling something herself, but sometimes you can feel things and not understand what it is you're feeling. I don't recall her ever saying anything about being exhausted or tired, so then eventually she began to have the start of a nervous breakdown.

"The statement she made on the Dick Clark show … That was a totally different type of show than some of the shows that we had been doing [locally]. It was very early in our career and anybody can make a mistake. I think overall, it was blown totally out of proportion. She said we were 'from Detroit, a suburb of Inkster,' which I'm sure … it was totally a mistake, but when someone asks you a question right then and there, we were new to the business and everybody can't think on his or her toes. That was *totally* an honest mistake. When she decided to respond to that particular question, which I think he had put the microphone more or less right in her face, you have to think on your toes right then and there. You don't always have time to think, even though on any given day, you know exactly where you're from. She could've been extremely nervous. We had done the local TV things in Detroit, but then here again, that was home. This was among your friends and some of your peers. [*American Bandstand*] was in Philadelphia. This was a national network, not a local one. Sometimes when you say things, you can think things and something else comes out of your mouth."

Gladys adds, "Inkster High School cancelled their football game because we were going to be on *American Bandstand* with 'Please Mr. Postman.' They were anxious to hear us mention Inkster, so they cancelled the game. When Dick Clark asked 'Where is Inkster, Michigan?' [Wyanetta], instead of saying 'Inkster is 30 miles outside of Detroit,' said 'Detroit is 30 miles outside of Inkster,' which still meant the same thing. She took it to heart because she knew those kids were waiting to hear the name Inkster. That put Wyanetta on a rocky road and she took it to heart. We said it was just a mistake and everyone laughed it off, but she didn't look at it like that. She looked at it as if it was the biggest mistake she ever made, which I'm sure she knows now that it wasn't."

Katherine continues, "Usually, Wyanetta was quiet. She would enjoy a lot of the fun that we may have been having, but she was usually quiet. She was always around people that you know. In the surroundings and comforts of your own environment, you often-times can be a totally different person. But when you're around a lot of strangers all the time, then it breaks down your security barriers. When you're around a lot of people that you don't know and you're working the kind of schedules that we were working, it can be totally exasperating. What people do not see is the amount of time that you spend away from your family or loved ones in order to do a finished product. There's a lot of work that goes into it prior to what the public sees as a finished product. There are hours and hours and days and days that go into rehearsing vocally and choreographically. There's just a lot of time that goes into it, so you may be scheduled to be home but in the scheduled period of time to be home, you're not on an R and R leave, you're home to work. You're trying to perform and perfect your art, your craft. Being away from your family for such long periods of time can be rather taxing."

A scapegoat was needed for allowing Wyanetta to be thrust into the entertainment field and a perfect one was found in Mrs. Sharpley, the student council advisor at Inkster High School who was responsible for securing the girls an audition at Motown.

She recalls, "After Wyanetta left the group because of the pressure and being away from home so much, I was blamed for pushing her into an arena that she shouldn't have been pushed into. I didn't know how widespread the condition was, but she more or less had a breakdown. It was a different world for youngsters from the small town of Inkster to all of a sudden be catapulted into nationwide recognition; being all dressed up, mingling with people who had made it ... That was something else for these children.

"It was rumored that she wouldn't have had the mental breakdown had she not been with the Marvelettes, and that hurt me; that really hurt me. In the teachers' lounge, you would hear, 'Yeah, Wyanetta never would've had the nervous breakdown had she not gone with the Marvelettes,' or 'Oh, yes, the Marvelettes. Mrs. Sharpley was responsible for them.' ... Word would get back to me. There wasn't anything I could say, I just endured it. People will talk. Small people always have a lot of talking to do. It was unfair, but small people have to have something to talk about. At that time, the Marvelettes were known countrywide, and Inkster is a very, very, small, gossipy type of town. So, I understood that."

Katherine retorts, "How can you find fault with someone who is trying to do good for you? In our case, [Mrs. Sharpley] was a teacher. If she had Wyanetta in a class, then she perhaps would've known better, but if she did not have her in any of her classes, then there was really no way. Mrs. Sharpley's primary thing was, 'Let's be fair about the [talent contest]. They were good, they were exceptionally good, so let's give them the benefit of the doubt.' I don't think it was a point of saying, 'Well, I don't think this person will make it.' You don't know who will and who won't. She, as well as Ms. Cobb, said, 'Hey, they were exceptionally good, so why not give them a chance, too.' Mrs. Sharpley was the more outspoken of the two. It just so happened that the fate of God was with us, and we were the ones that were chosen [by Motown]. Our time was right. I can't imagine Mrs. Sharpley being that kind of person. You don't know who will make it and who won't."

In the summer of 1962, the Marvelettes followed "Playboy" with "Beechwood 4-5789." Gladys sang lead on this chirpy tune where her character expresses a desire to date a particular guy. She'd like to get to know him better, so if he wants to dance with her or ask her for a date, he's more than welcome to at any time; thus, she gives him her phone number. The tune was written by Marvin Gaye (shortly before the release of his first hit single "Stubborn Kind of Fellow"), Mickey Stevenson, and Berry Gordy's brother, George. Stevenson handled "Beechwood"'s drum-laden production. However, the Marvelettes were on the road so much promoting their first three hits that when it came time to record the song, the group sang to a recorded track instead of behind live musicians. Katherine points out, "Motown had begun to start using recorded tracks because we were on the road an awful lot. I imagine the writer/producer had to get in the studio whenever they could get the time, and it would take a lot less time to have the recorded track already done than have us come in and do whatever we needed to do because, oftentimes, we were on a limited time span.

"We all realized that things changed, and we also realized that in many cases time was of the essence because if you were recording something, then if you had something that was released within that period, you also had to go and practice your choreography and all to prepare for doing a particular number on the stage, so oftentimes the time was of the essence. You may be home, but only be home for a week."

Gladys adds, "Berry wanted things fast, swift. Whoever wrote a song would come to us, find out if it was in the right key, then when we were on the road performing, they were in the studio. In the early days, Berry started a thing where the musicians would record the song, and the Andantes would do a lot of background work. Everybody would do the background vocals on tape. The music was already on. It just moved faster. If you could go in there, they could play a song for you on tape, you could put the words to it, that was quicker than having to set up the band, etc. ..."

"Beechwood 4-5789" may have had the Marvelettes singing to a recorded track; however, the excitement of singing behind live musicians was not lost on this release. When issued on July 11, 1962, "Beechwood 4-5789" followed the momentum of "Playboy" by hitting number seven on the *Billboard* R&B chart and number 17 on its pop listing. Katherine states, "I think a lot of the fans may very well have thought that [Beechwood 4-5789] was possibly one of our personal phone numbers. So then I'm sure there were several people that had the exchange of what 'Beechwood' would've been in different states that received numerous phone calls to the point in magnitude that they had to change their phone numbers. I'm thinking that at 15, 16, 17, very possibly it could be your fans trying to reach you in order to speak directly to you."

The Marvelettes released an album entitled *Playboy* in July 1962. Given the group's increased visibility since their debut eight months earlier, plus gradual changes in racial climate, the girls are pictured on the album's cover—the only LP to feature photos of all five original Marvelettes. Although Motown's Artist Development classes were still a few years away, the visual of *Playboy* reveals that some star grooming had taken place, as evidenced by the girls' stylish black dresses, particularly Wanda's low-cut outfit as she was quickly becoming the group's sex kitten. Katherine states, "I thought it was about time our photos were on the cover. I believe the climate was changing because we were performing a lot and everyone had pretty much seen us, so in seeing us, it was no longer a secret. It became more and more acceptable as time went on, whereas before it was somewhat taboo because many artists prior to us were not necessarily allowed the privilege of having their photos on the album because of the way racism was. You could like the music but don't distort the images."

Playboy was one of the group's finest efforts. In addition to the title song and "Beechwood 4-5789," the LP contained two standouts penned by the writing team of Brian Holland, Lamont Dozier, and Freddie Gorman: "Forever" and "Someday, Someway." The former was perhaps the Marvelettes' most memorable ballad. On "Forever," Wanda assumes the lead and delivers the lyrics in a sensual manner that was inarguably her finest vocal performance on vinyl up to that point; a complete departure from her somewhat annoying falsetto used on "So Long Baby." The song was produced by Brian Holland who, looking for an adult edge, kept the adolescent background vocals to a minimum and allowed Wanda free reign to turn this piano-driven track into her own tour de force. On "Forever," Wanda's character is willing to, among other things, allow herself to be played for a fool, tormented, and treated like a slave in return for her lover's affection.

A widely used publicity shot of the Marvelettes during their reign as Motown's premier girl group, circa 1962. (top) Gladys, Katherine (bottom) Wanda, Georgeanna. (Courtesy of Showtime Music Archives.)

"Wanda could make the men swoon with 'Forever,'" claims Martha Reeves.

"I think 'Forever' was a very nice love song," adds Katherine. "It talked about the love of two individuals and how one individual in particular would love the other individual forever. In some cases, for our 15-year-old and 16-year-old fans, it was a bit adultish. It was more of an adult-oriented type of song and not a teenager type of song. Adults could relate to it far better than the teenagers because in most cases, teenagers have felt puppy love but they never really felt a real love. And you didn't do that until you became an adult and you find that particular special person. Of course, when you're younger, you think you've found them but when you get older, you realize that you really haven't."

The mid-tempo, Latin-flavored "Someday, Someway" was the flip side of "Beechwood." Highlighted by its organ intro and Gladys' "wo-wo-wo" hooks, her character here expresses a desire to show her feelings for the guy she is singing to, but not until she is able to determine how committed he is to her. Gladys recalls, "I used to love to do 'Someday, Someway' on a show. We used to involve [bandleader] Choker Campbell, and he used to get involved in a little speech I did at the end."

Katherine adds, "'Someday, Someway' was like the beginning of a new relationship and someone having a crush on someone and thinking to themselves someday, someway you're going to let this person know how much you really love them." Despite being relegated to the flip side of "Beechwood," "Someday, Someway" reached number eight on the *Billboard* R&B chart in the fall of 1962.

Rounding out the album were two songs written by Berry Gordy himself: "I'm Hooked" and "(I've Got to) Cry Over You," the latter production borrowing heavily from the Shirelles' "Baby It's You"; "Mix It Up," a snappy, mid-tempo ditty written by Mickey Stevenson where Gladys' character uses the absence of her parents as an opportunity to throw a party; "I Think I Can Change You," a Smokey Robinson–penned ballad that had Gladys' character contemplating an attempt to straighten out a reputed "bad boy"; "Goddess of Love," a charming and exotic mid-tempo track led by Wanda and again written by Holland, Dozier, and Gorman; and the ballad "You Should Know," which had Gladys singing several octaves above her natural voice.

CHAPTER 5

Motortown Revue

I n the summer of 1962, Motown began planning its first Motortown Revue Tour, which was a series of concert dates that would take place from the end of October until mid-December. The plan behind the Revue was to send all of the label's artists out on the road, promote the company, further boost the more recognized acts, provide exposure for the unknown artists, and generate money to offset the slow payment from record distributors. The Revue was the brainchild of Esther Edwards and Thomas "Beans" Bowles. A native of South Bend, Indiana, Bowles was a saxophonist, flutist, and arranger, who began working professionally at age 16. He moved to Detroit in 1944 to study at Wayne State University. Shortly afterward, Bowles left school and played in a U.S. Navy band that performed nationally and abroad. Upon his return to Detroit, he worked at many jazz bars, including Sonny Wilson's Forest Club, the 20 Grand, and the Flame Show Bar. It was at the Flame where Bowles met Berry Gordy, whose sister Gwen owned a photo concession there and where another sister, Anna, also worked. This association would lead to Bowles becoming one of Motown's original session musicians, debuting on Marv Johnson's 1959 hit single "Come to Me." He would later become a member of the label's management company, ITMI, as he impressed everyone with his knowledge of show business and his ideas on how to enhance live performances.

Motown affiliated itself with Supersonic Attractions, headed by promoter Henry Wynne, who was also black. Wynne's connections in the South were strong, and he was a welcome ally for a new label with an inability to find reputable booking agents to arrange concert dates. The Revue featured the Miracles, Mary Wells, the Marvelettes, the Temptations, Marv Johnson, Stevie Wonder, the Contours, Marvin Gaye, Martha (Reeves) and the Vandellas, the Supremes, and Singing Sammy Ward. Despite a time when only the Miracles, the Marvelettes, Mary Wells, Marv Johnson, and the Contours (thanks to their recently released smash "Do You Love Me") could be considered drawing cards, Motown was able to convince the promoter to book its entire company roster.

Forty-five artists and musicians (who had been organized by the house bandleader, Choker Campbell), chaperones for the girl groups, and other administrative personnel would make the trek in five cars and a dilapidated bus that had no bathroom facilities. However, these conditions seemed minor to most of the young artists who were too excited about their burgeoning careers and the freedom that came with leaving home for the first time.

Martha Reeves recalls, "Every Monday there was a company meeting and the artists were invited along with the staff. They would sit there and try to figure out how to make Motown a better place. They would field questions and queries that the artists had. In some of the meetings we were given instructions as to whose record was going to come out and who was scheduled to go on the road.

"They called us in and said, 'Well, we have a tour and Thomas "Beans" Bowles is going to be the tour manager, and we're going to have the following acts ...' And when they named all of these acts, I was thrilled. When they said how long we were going to be gone, it didn't really matter because I had no responsibilities. I was free to go and do what I've always dreamed of doing, being onstage and touring. This was better than I had dreamed because I was with such wonderful stars that had led the way. The Miracles' hits were hopping all over the United States and people were starting to call 'Beechwood 4-5789.' "

Katherine adds, "We were all relatively excited because the Motortown Revue was not too many months after we had started and came out, and the tour allowed for all of the Motown artists to be seen by more than just the people in Washington, Maryland, Chicago, and New York. It gave many of the southern as well as the north and northeast cities the opportunity to see the artists of Motown.

"[The traveling] wasn't a life of luxury that these young people have now. It was extremely uncomfortable, it was extremely crowded; but considering it all, you had a lot of fun because you were able to set up your friendships with your co-workers."

The tour began at the Howard Theater in Washington, D.C. After a performance in Boston on November 2, the schedule of the tour was mind-boggling as the Revue played 16 straight one-nighters.

DAY	DATE	CITY & STATE	PLACE OF ENGAGEMENT
Fri.	11/2/62	Boston, MA	Franklin Theater
Sat.	11/3/62	New Haven, CT	New Haven Arena
Sun.	11/4/62	Buffalo, NY	Memorial Auditorium
Mon.	11/5/62	Raleigh, NC	Raleigh City Auditorium
Tues.	11/6/62	Charleston, SC	County Hall
Wed.	11/7/62	Augusta, GA	Country Club
Thurs.	11/8/62	Savannah, GA	Bamboo Ranch Club
Fri.	11/9/62	Birmingham, AL	City Auditorium
Sat.	11/10/62	Columbus, GA	City Auditorium
Sun.	11/11/62	Atlanta, GA	Magnolia Ballroom
Mon.	11/12/62	Mobile, AL	Fort Whiting Auditorium
Tues.	11/13/62	New Orleans, LA	State Fairgrounds
Wed.	11/14/62	Jackson, MS	College Park Auditorium
Thurs.	11/15/62	Spartansburg, SC	Memorial Auditorium
Fri.	11/16/62	Durham, NC	City Armory
Sat.	11/17/62	Columbia, SC	Township Auditorium
Sun.	11/18/62	Washington, DC	Capitol Arena
Mon.	11/19/62	DAY OFF	

The Miracles had limited tour experience. However, most of the artists, particularly the girl groups, had yet to perfect a stage act. Katherine points out, "Contrary to what has been said of when they talk about Artist Development and Maxine Powell teaching charm, which of course she did do, and Cholly Atkins doing choreography, and the vocal coaches and all of that ... that did not occur until around 1964. We had already been out there.

"Most of the choreography of the earlier years came through the talent of the artists. We did our own choreography in each other's homes. We didn't have a rehearsal hall or rehearsal room in the earlier years of Motown. We did it in each other's homes. There was no code of ethics as to what should or should not occur, and we were literally thrown out there. We did do the little record hops and things and the local offerings. On one interview, Beans Bowles made the comment—and he was making the comment more or less comical or making it seem as though it were comical —in regards to Georgeanna coming out on stage chewing gum. Yes, it was improper, but there was no one there to say, 'Well, you're not supposed to go out there with gum in your mouth,' which should have been a given. And if you slipped up and did do it, then you don't criticize them for it. If anything, you say that that's not appropriate. But when you go out there to perform, you don't really know because you *are* only high school kids, and you are inexperienced. You don't have anyone to advise you as to what to do. We were literally thrown out there to the wolves and they said, 'Here, do it and make the best of it.'

"Overall, the Marvelettes' performances generally went over very well. Very seldom were we criticized to the point of, 'You shouldn't do this, you shouldn't do that.' There was additional grooming that was necessary as far as performing because, in actuality, you did good to figure out how to get on and off the damn stage. There really wasn't anyone to tell you."

Not only did the tour have problems with performers being relatively new to the stage, but the Motortown Revue was the first time many of the younger artists had been in the South; and thus, their first experience with segregation. For some, it was the first time they had ever been refused entry to a hotel or had to use a "blacks-only" bathroom. This was nothing new for veteran black artists who had performed in the South and were denied adequate dining and sleeping facilities, or appropriate arrangements where they performed.

The Crystals, an all-black female quintet from New York, were riding high in the early 1960s with hits "Uptown," "He's a Rebel," "Da Do Ron Ron," and "Then He Kissed Me." Thus, they met the inevitable demand for touring in the South. Lead singer Delores "La La" Brooks recalls the struggle of being a young black female entertainer on the road. "We had it rough," she says. "The sleeping quarters and buses were horrible. Most of the time it would be an old-fashioned bus and most of them didn't have a bathroom. If they did, they weren't made for a month-and-a-half or two-month tour where they were continuously used. The bathroom was so cluttered and the toilet stopped up. Sometimes you couldn't go to the bathroom in certain towns because of the racism. We'd have to just hold going to the toilet until we got to the next town. That was difficult because I remember sitting on the bus and going up to the bus driver and asking him, 'My God, when are we going to get to the next town?!' We had hard times and it made us harder and it made us stronger. We had a lot of stress and strain at a young age on tour.

"The strain wasn't only physical, it was mental. Performance-wise we had strain because of the dressing rooms. We weren't allowed to dress in the dressing rooms; we dressed in the kitchen. I remember dressing in the kitchen many a day. My group would form a circle around me so I could change. I would be in the middle and I'd slip on my dress. As each one changed we would cover them with our bodies. After we dressed, someone would bring us through the kitchen and to the stage. Then he would stand on the side of the stage to bring us back through the kitchen after we finished. Even when we ate, we weren't allowed to eat in the restaurants or the clubs wherever we played. We had to get into the car and go to the next gig. If we were hungry in places where we could enter after we left the show, we weren't allowed to go into the front, we'd have to go around back and sit in the car and the girl would come around and take our order. We were back there in the garbage area, and while waiting for our order, you could see the rats jumping on the garbage cans because it was nighttime, and that's where they would throw the garbage.

"You would say to yourself, 'Damn, I just finished performing for these people. We can't even eat in their restaurants, we can't go to their toilets, we can't go anyplace but just do the gig and leave.' "

The Motown artists would endure similar treatment. The Revue took place at a time when there was an increase in civil rights protests, sit-ins, and demonstrations. Just a year earlier, Freedom Riders — black and white college students from the North — flocked South in buses and cars similar to the one carrying the Motown crew. The bus's Michigan license plates stood out on Southern highways like a sore thumb.

When the Motortown bus broke down in Macon, Georgia, a local service station refused to help with repairs. At a motel in South Carolina, the white guests vacated the swimming pool as soon as the Motown troupe arrived in their swimsuits. In Montgomery, Alabama, the driver found bullets embedded in the Motortown Revue sign on the front of the bus.

Katherine notes, "I was exposed to quite a bit as a child growing up, and our big vacation was usually for us to go to the South where my grandparents lived. My grandfather had a farm. When they went into town, not too often did the kids go into town, but if we did we were pre-instructed that if a white person speaks to you, it's 'yes, sir,' 'yes, ma'am,' don't do this, don't do that. One time I did have the opportunity to go into town and I spoke out of turn, and my grandfather was right there defending me and saying that I was from the North and I didn't know any better. However, although I had been in the South, I had never experienced the racism to the magnitude that I did when I went on the Motown tour. It's a different ballgame when you're in a little country town because all you're going to, and all you're visiting is that little small country town. However, when you're visiting many of the major cities in the South, then the experiences are greater. And it became very, very ... frightening. You would do these tours and travel down the highway when the whites saw you and they saw your bus, which was like a Greyhound type of bus, they began to think that we were Freedom Riders. Of course, we had our banner stating that we were from Motown, but they did think we were Freedom Riders. And they responded in that very negative way that many people heard about and didn't believe that it was true. We all feared for our lives. Hell, when somebody's acting like they're getting ready to turn your bus over and they start shooting at you ... you don't know what's going to happen.

"My parents oftentimes saw to it that we had different black publications that were available at that time. There was *Jet* and I remember seeing the *Pittsburgh Courier*. You had a chance to read about some of these things. But to read about them and to experience them, it's totally different. I don't think my parents or any of the other parents had any idea of what we went through or encountered. I personally would often call my mother from the road or send a postcard, but I never went into explaining the fear of what transpired because I know she would've been a nervous wreck."

Annette Beard Helton of the Vandellas adds "We got firsthand what it was like to be black in the South, and that was something that was totally new to us. We had heard about things in school and from the papers and things of that nature, but to actually go through some of those experiences was really quite shocking for us because we had never heard of two different water faucets and bathrooms that said 'colored.' We had prejudices here in the North but not like down there. It was a whole new awakening.

"We went through a lot of things that were totally out of character for us. To not be able to walk into a restaurant and order food from the front; blacks had to go to the back. It was like, 'What?!' And to not be able to use bathrooms, even in the bus stations. Our driver was white, so he was able to go into the bus station and buy food for us, but it was something we could not have imagined."

Most of the theaters in which the artists performed were segregated with whites seated on the floor levels and blacks in the balconies, or with whites on one side of the theater and blacks on the other. If there were no balcony, a rope would be put in place from the center stage straight down the aisle to the back of the theater: blacks on one side of the rope, whites on the other.

"These are things that stay with you for the rest of your life," contends Katherine. "You're young, you're impressionable, and it's rather hard to perform to an audience where the whites are on the floor and the blacks are in the balcony. There may be a rope to keep the blacks from coming down. You may have a full house, but it was rather disheartening as black people to see other black people behind banisters of the balcony. And they're enjoying your music as well as white people but because of the times, they were not able to enjoy it as much.

"I think most of us took the attitude that, 'We'll just go out here and perform to the best of our ability and try our best not to let it affect us as much as it may have.' You try to do a good show but the bottom line is, your heart's racing because you don't know what is going to occur because you're in a whole, totally different area. It's like being abandoned, on your own in the middle of nowhere, and not being able to see rescuers for a good little while. We didn't feel that we were going to have that much support as far as rescuers if it came down to it. We had to try to protect ourselves."

"When the other groups went onstage, we weren't in our dressing rooms, we were always backstage or to the side of the stage," says Annette Helton. "The support was always on both sides; stage left and stage right. It was so strange what was going on in front of us. To be able to look to both sides and see your own and know they felt the same way you did, helped a lot."

Martha Reeves adds, "We couldn't move unless there were two or three [local] people who knew the people that were going around and could be accepted or get through. There was always someone who kind of escorted you through the perils that you went through. We weren't instructed or had no idea that kind of racism existed. I knew I was born in the South and I knew that if you didn't say 'yes, sir' and 'no, sir' in some areas, they would kill you. A lot of things were happening that put us in a danger spot."

Bowles served as the tour's road manager and was responsible for collecting the money, which could amount to over $15,000 a night. He and driver Eddie McFarland would travel a day early to the next city to monitor ticket sales and hotel availability. Tragedy struck the tour on Thanksgiving Day 1962 when Bowles and McFarland had an accident en route from North Carolina to Florida. Apparently, McFarland stayed up late the night before and had too much to drink at a company party. As a result, he fell asleep at the wheel and crashed their white station wagon into the back of a truck. McFarland was hospitalized in critical condition for three days before he died. Bowles had been in the back of the station wagon practicing his flute and on impact, the instrument plunged through his armpit and came out through the back of his neck. He was in critical condition with two broken legs and doctors predicted he would never walk again. Miraculously, Bowles made a nearly full recovery.

Hours after the accident, the Revue bus came upon the mangled car. With both passengers missing, they continued on to Florida. Upon arrival, they received a telegram stating that Esther Edwards was on her way to Florida to supervise the rest of the tour. When she arrived, she informed the artists and musicians of the fate of Bowles and McFarland.

"Eddie McFarland was basically [the Marvelettes'] driver," recalls Katherine. "He traveled mostly with us and he drove us when we started out. His death affected us quite a bit and as you look at it, now you understand how fragile a life is. Today you see someone and they're happy-go-lucky, and then the next day you're made aware that they had a tragic accident and he had lost his life. I think [the Marvelettes] were really affected. I believe everybody else was, also, but we felt it even more because we knew him better. With Beans, the word that we were getting was that he would never play his instrument and I think my thought at the time was, 'What a tragic loss for someone, such a fine musician, to not be able to ever play his instrument again.' But God is good because he was able to play his instrument again. He was able to do any number of things. He was even able to teach as life went on. He pretty much fully recovered from the accident."

After twelve one-nighters in thirteen days, the tour finally ended with a ten-day engagement at the Apollo Theater in Harlem. A drab building of five floors of tiny, dreary dressing rooms, the Apollo nevertheless was one of the most famous presentations in the world and was usually the dream of most young black entertainers. However, Harlem's audiences were known to be brutally frank. If they liked you, you knew it, and if they did not like you, you also knew it by the booing and hissing, and occasionally having things thrown at you. As a result, it was often stated that if you can make it at the Apollo, you can make it anywhere. All of the Motown artists were equally as nervous and excited about the opportunity to play the Apollo.

Katherine recalls, "When we first went to the Apollo, the Apollo had such a bad name in the business. We were petrified because veteran performers said, 'Well, if you go to the Apollo and you're no good, you get booed off the stage, they throw food at you...' whatever, all of those kinds of things. Well, when you have young people 16, 17 years old, it was like, 'Oh, my God. I don't know if I ever want to get there,' but to get to the Apollo and to make it... my thing was, after a period of time, you'd get to the Apollo and you do well at the Apollo, then you should not have any fear of performing anywhere else. I would say New York, Harlem people, if you can make it through them, you can make it through *anything*. They let you know whether or not you're a good performer. After awhile, we began to visit the Apollo so much and we began to develop friendships. The owner of the Apollo, we looked forward to seeing him, and seeing Honi Coles, and moving from *way* up top in the dressing room status down to the lower dressing room. When you become the headliner, then you get dressing rooms on the lower floor. But if you were new and an upstart, then you had to go up far more steps.

"The most important thing we were considering was making sure that we were really good because we didn't want to go through that being booed off the stage. That was our basic thing, just making sure that we were really good in what we did. Fortunately, we were; we were very well accepted in New York at the Apollo. We were there so often that [owner] Bobby Schiffman or Honi would come over and say, 'Kat, we'd like for you to do the announcement.' Oftentimes, I was the backstage person making the announcement of the up-and-coming shows. Not only did I do it there, but I did it in D.C. [at the Howard Theater]."

By the time the tour ended with a December 17 date in Pittsburgh, everyone was glad to be back in Detroit in time for Christmas. "Regardless of how many people you met, friends and relationships you established, coming home and being home for the holidays is the best," says Katherine. "Most of the times we were able to take it and spend time with our families but in most cases, too, we were going to the Fox Theater. That allowed for all of us —the Motown stable of artists—to be with our families while performing at the Fox Theater. We were at the Fox pretty much every holiday. Motown would usually have us close, near home, working."

CHAPTER 6

The Lull

T he year 1962 proved to be the finale of the Marvelettes' reign as Motown's number one girl group. On October 29, 1962, they released "Strange I Know," featuring Gladys on lead. A song slightly slower than moderate, "Strange I Know" was the Marvelettes' first A-side that was not up-tempo; a change of pace that was utilized primarily to add some diversity to the group's live performances. Katherine explains, "A lot of our B-sides were slow songs, so it was very possible that 'Strange I Know' just flipped the coin from being the up-tempo side to the slow side. There was just absolutely no way you could've done—whatever your time period was—a lot of up-tempo songs. You had to be able to slow it down some in order to, if nothing else, get your breath. We did a lot of steps and routines, so we would need to slow the pace down, just to gather ourselves."

"Strange I Know" was an "out-of-sight-out-of-mind" tune that was written by the team of Brian Holland (who also produced it), Freddie Gorman, and Lamont Dozier, and was perhaps something of a finale to the "Please Mr. Postman" story. Here, Gladys' character has fallen out of love with a faraway boyfriend. While he is away, she meets a new man who she now plans to marry. Although her actions are justified because the previous boyfriend hadn't bothered to write or call, there is still a heavy trace of guilt in Gladys' voice as she sings the lyrics, perhaps because she left her "Dear John" letter to him with her mother. Led by its distinctive guitar intro, "Strange I Know" was popular with the black audience and reached number 10 on *Billboard*'s R&B chart early in 1963.

However, after being handed an up-tempo diet of "Please Mr. Postman," "Twistin' Postman," "Playboy," and "Beechwood 4-5789," mainstream radio was not quite ready for a moderately slow tune from the Marvelettes, as "Strange I Know" stalled at number 49 on the pop listing; the group's first single that failed to crack the *Billboard* pop top 40.

The girls followed in the spring of 1963 with "Locking Up My Heart," featuring trade-off leads by Gladys and Wanda; the latter in her "So Long Baby"–ish falsetto. Here, our heroines have been hurt by love so many times they refuse to love again. Both Gladys and Wanda sing the lyrics in a defiant manner; content with having conquered heartache and knowing it will not happen again. It is this defiance that allows for "Locking Up My Heart" to have an upbeat, dramatic flavor. This horn-dominated tune was particularly noteworthy because it was the first A-side to feature writing credits by Brian Holland, Lamont Dozier, and Eddie Holland, the songwriting and production team that would greatly define the Motown sound for much of the decade. Unfortunately for the Marvelettes, Holland-Dozier-Holland had yet to find their niche, as "Locking Up My Heart" was only moderately successful, reaching number 25 on the *Billboard* R&B chart and number 44 on the pop listing. Motown chose to place "Forever" onto the flip side of "Locking Up My Heart." The former received airplay at the same time and charted, reaching number 24 on the *Billboard* R&B chart but bottoming out at number 78 on the pop side. It has been argued that by the two songs receiving dual airplay, they cancelled each other out in sales.

"As Motown was releasing different things, sometimes they somewhat killed their own records," states Katherine. "If you had something that was still moving or going up the charts, and if they see that it may be dropping just a tad, then they would throw something else out there. That means it will kill the one that was already there because it would have to make room for the one that was just released."

Nevertheless, "Locking Up My Heart" was particularly popular when the Marvelettes performed live and was usually the song that ended their set. Having Gladys and Wanda alternate leads on the song allowed for the Marvelettes to put together a spectacularly choreographed act featuring Katherine and Georgeanna moving in tight unison with Wanda while Gladys opened the song and then, without missing a beat, switching to Gladys as Wanda assumed the lead. However, the highlight of their performance was Wanda stretching out the finale, in which she sang like a woman possessed; scatting, ad-libbing such lines as "You should've treated me right. I wouldn't have had to cry" and "Just love me a little. I wouldn't have had to sigh," and often "working" the front row of the audience. " 'Locking Up My Heart' was our showstopper," claims Gladys. "Wanda used to wear that song out at the end. She would get with the policeman, or whoever was down front in the audience. She would sing to them and the audience went wild."

For the song, each girl wore a mechanical heart on her dress, illuminated by a red spotlight that would beat in time to the music. Katherine remembers, "I used to shop at a store called Paraphernalia during that particular time, and it was a high-end trendy kind of shop. I had gone in there to get something and I saw this particular dress; a mini-dress that had long sleeves to it. What was unique about this mini-dress was that it had a heart on it that pulsated. We could go into one pocket and turn it on and the heart pulsated. I thought it was so cute. I had the other girls come in and look at it to see what they thought about it. When we performed 'Locking Up My Heart,' [the pulsating heart] freaked out a lot of the audiences. They often wondered what we were going to do next."

In the summer of 1963, the Marvelettes released "My Daddy Knows Best," written by Berry Gordy. Gladys sang lead on this moderately paced tune with a typical girl-group theme. Here, her character's father has warned her to not be blinded by love; that many would-be suitors would tell her the sweet things she wanted to hear, only to come with broken promises. Realizing that her father is right, she tells the particular guy to whom she sings to spend more time in schoolrooms instead of poolrooms, and to get a job. "My Daddy Knows Best" only reached number 67 on the *Billboard* pop chart and, surprisingly, missed the R&B chart entirely. All three singles were included on the group's album entitled *The Marvelous Marvelettes*, released February 28, 1963.

Motown normally made it a practice to link its artists with specific producers in hopes of spawning a successful, creative marriage. However, as evident with this LP, virtually everyone had a hand in producing the Marvelettes. Brian Holland was responsible for "Strange I Know" and its flip side, the popular "Too Strong to Be Strung Along." Holland also teamed with Dozier for the production of "Locking Up My Heart." Berry Gordy was responsible for

Hit-making stars of the girl group phenomenon.
(L–R) Gladys, Georgeanna, Wanda, Katherine.
(Courtesy of Showtime Music Archives)

"My Daddy Knows Best." New York native up-and-coming writer/ producer Norman Whitfield generated the melancholy "Why Must You Go" and "Silly Boy," the latter on which each Marvelette had a phrase to sing. Whitfield also teamed with Mickey Stevenson to produce "It's Gonna Take a Lot of Doing (To Undo All the Damage That You've Done)." Stevenson single-handedly produced three of the album's tracks: "I Forgot About You," "Which Way Did He Go," and "Smart Aleck." Although several writers and producers took part in *The Marvelous Marvelettes*, there were some patterns of consistency: Gladys sang lead on all ten of the album's tracks, and the overall theme was one of her character having the upper hand in relationships with boys, or at the very least, being aware of a potential suitor trying to pull the wool over her eyes. The only tracks that had her character showing any vulnerability were "It's Gonna Take a Lot of Doing (To Undo All the Damage That You've Done)" and "Why Must You Go."

One of the group's more popular songs at this time was "Tie a String Around Your Finger," which was the flip side of "My Daddy Knows Best." Gladys assumes the lead on this ballad that featured chimes. Here, as her character prepares to go away, she tells her boyfriend that she still loves him. In return, she asks that he remain faithful. In addition, she asks that he tie a string around his finger to remind him of her love. "Tie a String Around Your Finger" would later become an integral part of the Marvelettes' live show, using such props as strings and neon gloves. Katherine recalls, "We had neon-sprayed gloves or white gloves that we used with a black light. So, in most cases, you would not see us, the artists, but you would see the choreography of the gloves by using the black light, and we went through the hand motions so that it appeared that we were indeed tying a string."

Curiously, "Tie a String Around Your Finger" was excluded from *The Marvelous Marvelettes* LP. Equally curious was that Gladys sang lead instead of Wanda. It was a bit of a stretch for Gladys to sing lyrics reminding a boyfriend of her love and kisses, and *pleading* with him to remain faithful while she was gone. She normally assumed the role of a strong-willed individual who took no mess and would tell a boyfriend about himself if he did decide to stray. Wanda, on the other hand, had a softer, more vulnerable dimension in her voice and was better suited to pledge her love to a boyfriend, similar to what she did on "Forever." Although there was no official announcement, it was clear that Gladys would be singing lead on all Marvelettes' songs during this period.

Later that year the group released a live set entitled *The Marvelettes on Stage, Recorded Live*, which was recorded at the Regal Theater in Chicago. The album reprised many of their hits— "Beechwood 4-5789," a medley of "Strange I Know" and "Someday, Someway," which featured a monologue by Gladys, "Locking Up My Heart," "Twistin' Postman," "So Long Baby," "Playboy"—and a cover of Bobby Lewis' 1961 Number One smash "Tossing and Turning." Curiously, "Please Mr. Postman" was not part of this set. The LP proved that Gladys and Wanda were not the result of studio magic but sounded the same in person. The album's high points were a highly enthusiastic and vocal audience, endearing, yet somewhat out-of-tune background vocals, and a great band.

Katherine notes, "We had hits, no doubt about it, but to be able to present these hits in duplication, we had to have musicians, and the ones we had were very good. Giving them their props is no more than right. Our first guitar player, Eddie Willis, was a Motown musician. The one who stuck with us through thick and thin was Johnny Gilliam, who was from Pittsburgh. He would hang in there with me. Then we had another musician whose name was Norman Roberts out of Philadelphia. He was our drummer and a very talented young man. He worked with us for a couple of years, then he left and was involved with the Temptations. We had another one, whose name was Gregory, and he was out of Norfolk, Virginia. He was our drummer after Norman. He didn't stay out there with us for too long, either. Johnny Gilliam was the one who stuck with us all the way through the end."

The Marvelettes toured constantly and were regulars on the so-called "chitlin' circuit," particularly on the East Coast; consistently appearing at such predominantly African-American–patronized clubs as the Apollo Theater in Harlem, the Uptown

The Marvelettes' most famous photo as a quartet.
(L–R) Gladys, Wanda, Georgeanna, Katherine.
(author's collection)

Theater in Philadelphia, the Royal Theater in Baltimore, the Howard Theater in Washington D.C., and the Regal Theater in Chicago. "The East Coast was just our thing," claims Katherine. "Philly, Washington, Baltimore... They were just our towns when we got there. The actual clubs were basically the same. It was the people in the areas that made it different. In Philadelphia, we would go to eat at someone's home that was [located near the] back of the Uptown. She would prepare food for everyone on the show. Everyone would meet over there and she would have some luxurious smothered pork chops and smothered chicken. It was like an open kitchen. In Baltimore and Washington, you could go right out of the theater door and you're somewhere where you could eat. You could not do that at the Apollo. You would have to go a little distance, and it was the same at the Regal in Chicago.

"With the kind of time slots that we were often working in, we would be together all day long. When we performed at theaters such as the Apollo, or the Howard, or the Regal, then we would be doing, in most cases, five shows a day. Through the week you would have more time [to yourself] than you would on the weekend. When it came to the weekends, which consisted of Friday, Saturday, and Sunday, we may have been doing seven. On the weekends, you busted your butt. Your day would start very, very early, and it would end very, very late. As we matured and we were making more money, we would have our own individual rooms, but earlier in our career we were sharing rooms. Many times when the show was over, we would stop to get something to eat if there was something open, then we would go to our rooms, probably eat our food, and then take a bath and just crash until the next day."

Brenda Holloway, who worked numerous gigs with the Marvelettes, adds, "Being on the road was tedious. We were younger, but it was very tedious because it took all of our day. We didn't have any social life when we were performing. It took the better part of the day and the evening. All we were ready for was bed whenever we got finished. So, it was very … it was kind of tedious for us. It seemed to be harder for us than for the men. We had so many wigs and so many costumes and so much sibling rivalry among some of the female acts. They were a bit catty. The men were nice. They kind of stayed to themselves. They had their own agenda. Women, we basically were together all day long; learning makeup tricks from each other, just being with each other. We were with each other *a lot.*

"I liked the Marvelettes. They seemed to be down to earth. Wanda was almost the most beautiful woman I had ever seen. They seemed to be really, really down to earth. They were more like regular home girls.

"Their stage act was fabulous. They were tight. They worked hard on their craft and they were good. I remember one gig at the

Uptown with Jerry Butler, Patti Labelle, the Marvelettes, and myself. The Marvelettes were *very* popular there. They should have been the headliners on that show."

Onstage is where the Marvelettes really shined, and where they would build a reputation as arguably Motown's most dynamic female group. Although contributions came from everyone, Gladys was responsible for the majority of the group's stage act.

"Everyone had some input into what we did onstage," she says. "I did a lot of the routines, especially after Katherine and Wanda were married and I was still single. I had a lot of time to listen to the songs and make up steps and teach them. We were just a group where if I said, 'This is what we're going to do onstage,' they would watch and they would learn. It wasn't a thing where someone would question it. If, for example, Wanda came up with something better, we would do that. Wanda had a lot to do with the wardrobe because she loved clothes. The Marvelettes always thought of something different. I knew that we couldn't just do a song and end it."

Martha Reeves points out, "In the very beginning, the Marvelettes were co-starring because they had the biggest hits. Motown kept you on your toes, and the Marvelettes led it because they were the twirlers and the spinners. They were the Temptations of the girls. They did wonderful moves; they were show people. They had lovely costumes and they had nice legs. You could see that Wanda and Gladys had nice legs. They danced and showed their legs."

Eddie Willis, a guitarist in Motown's legendary studio band, the Funk Brothers, continues, "When the Marvelettes went out there, they were well respected. The whole theater would be hitting on them. In every theater we played, every guy would be trying to get close enough to say 'Hi' to them. The audiences *loved* them. What really stood out was when they played the Apollo Theater. That was the proven ground. If you go in there, do your thing, come out, and people are at the back [entrance] of the theater giving you cheers, you did okay. I saw that with the Marvelettes.

"It seemed like they had two or three special places. New York was one and Philadelphia was *definitely* one. In Philly, it seemed like that audience was waiting for them. If the Marvelettes were there three months ago, the fans felt that it had been too long; they should've been back after a month and a half."

The live album was the Marvelettes' fifth LP in two years; a clear indication of Motown trying to milk the group's success while they were still one of the label's premier acts. Katherine points out, "The most important thing about us was that, 'The girls are hot. Let's see what we can get out on them next. Since they more or less have fans and have a following, let's see how fast we can get another record out on them. Let's try to get as many out as we possibly can because we don't know how long this is going to last.' "

As the Marvelettes saw their 1963 singles fail to reach the lofty heights of their songs from the previous year, and they were shifted around from one producer to another, Martha and the Vandellas replaced them as Motown's top girl group. Lead singer Martha Reeves already had some seasoning by the time she came to Motown. As the tenor of a female quartet called the Del-Phis, she gained experience in the studio, backing up local soul singers J. J. Barnes and Mike Hanks, and the group cut a single of their own in 1961 for the Check-mate label, Chess Records' Detroit-based affiliate. Reeves went to Motown to audition as a singer, but was instead offered a job as A&R secretary to Mickey Stevenson, a position she accepted. Having gotten her foot in the door at Motown, Reeves was able to bring in her fellow group members, Annette Beard, Rosalind Ashford, and original lead singer Gloria Williamson, for work as session background singers on Motown recordings. Among their most notable sessions were backing Marvin Gaye on "Stubborn Kind of Fellow," "Hitch Hike," and "Pride and Joy."

The group also got a chance to record a single of their own. Since they were still under contract as the Del-Phis, Motown changed their name to the Vells for the 1962 release of "You'll Never Cherish a Love So New" backed with "There He Is (At My Door)" on its Mel-O-Day subsidiary. Williamson sang lead on the song, but after it failed to make any noise, she dropped out of the group to take a job with the city of Detroit and raise her two children.

Reeves was then enlisted to sing lead. When Mary Wells failed to show up for a recording session for a tune called "I'll Have to Let Him Go," Reeves called the rest of the girls to the studio to record the song. Berry Gordy then instructed the trio to come up with a new permanent name. The moniker Vandellas was created when Reeves combined Van Dyke Avenue with that of the singer Della Reese.

Martha and the Vandellas scored with three consecutive hits in 1963 and reigned as Motown's premier female group (L–R) Martha Reeves, Annette Beard, Rosalind Ashford.
(author's collection)

"I'll Have to Let Him Go" was released by Martha and the Vandellas in the fall of 1962 and sank without a trace. Despite this setback, Motown still saw the group as a potentially viable act. They were paired with the Holland-Dozier-Holland team for "Come and Get These Memories," a tune that was recorded in 1962 but would not be released as a single until February 22, 1963. In the interim, Martha and the Vandellas performed the song everywhere they could, while traveling with Marvin Gaye to promote "Stubborn Kind of Fellow." They also had the opportunity to perform "Come and Get These Memories" on *American Bandstand*, a marketing strategy that paid off. After Motown finally released the single, it had instant recognition among listeners and became a hit. "Come and Get These Memories" reached number six on the *Billboard* R&B chart in the spring of 1963 and made the pop top 30. Later that summer the Vandellas and H-D-H achieved national prominence with "(Love Is Like A) Heat Wave." "Heat Wave," a tune that Reeves vocally tore up, sat atop the *Billboard* R&B chart for four weeks and crossed over to number four on the pop chart. The group maintained its momentum when "Quicksand," a "Heat Wave" sound-alike, was nearly as well-received as its predecessor upon its release in the fall. With three straight hits, Martha and the Vandellas were suddenly at the forefront of Motown's growing empire. As their success came at a time when the Marvelettes were hitting a lull, many observers saw it as something of a passing of the torch.

"You could feel [the lull]," recalls Katherine. "Maybe no one knew what direction they wanted to take us. Whatever we recorded was directed primarily by the producers, or Berry, or whoever would be in charge. So if they weren't trying to move us in a certain direction, we had no say-so and no control over that. I figured our job was to perform and do the best that we could. Their job was to keep a good product in order to keep us working.

"As far as recording, there was enough for everybody. The country and the world were large enough and the company was growing, so you could accommodate [the Marvelettes and the Vandellas]. I thought our music and their music, though alike, was very different. However, as time went on, it was almost like, 'Well, [the Marvelettes] can pretty much carry themselves.' It seemed as though they were putting more into the other artists than they were into us."

In contrast to the teenage image of the Marvelettes, Martha and the Vandellas were presented as more adult, given how they were in their early 20s when they had their breakthrough with "Come and Get These Memories." In retrospect, this tune is a bit tame compared to "Heat Wave" and "Quicksand"; the latter two songs containing the energetic, gospel-infused, tambourine-charged arrangement that would set Martha and the Vandellas apart from the other female groups at Motown.

The Marvelettes never felt threatened by the presence of Martha and the Vandellas. On the contrary, they were quite supportive in helping the Vandellas make the transition from obscurity to one of the country's leading acts.

Martha Reeves recalls, "I first met the Marvelettes when I was A&R secretary and I was answering the phone. Gladys called and I answered 'Martha Reeves, A&R Department.' She said, 'Girl, there ain't no A&R secretary.' I said, 'Yes there is … today,' because I didn't know how long I was going to be there. I was just answering the phone. She said, 'Girl, I'm coming down there. I've got to see you.' And it was comical because I was in the process of calling her to tell her about a session they had scheduled. She was just surprised that it was me on the phone. When I got to meet her, she was delightful. I got to know her really well and when the other girls came in, they were delightful as well. They were fun-loving. You couldn't find any nicer girls.

"Wanda was always a character. Wanda would always say things to make you laugh. She had a very, very good sense of humor … She was sort of quiet. You had to go to her to get her to say something. She was sort of quiet and into herself.

"The biggest thrill and the camaraderie began with the Marvelettes and Martha and the Vandellas when we first went on the first tour and we weren't ready for it. We had our record out but we didn't know whether it was going to be a hit or not. We had performed locally as the Del-Phis, but had never gone on any stage shows like what we were faced with. We had a few little [outfits] that were sewn by our mothers and different friends who were so-called seamstresses, but the Marvelettes had some nice things. Gladys went and got four of their costumes, and I could chose from the four of them and get three that were similar to our size. I made the adjustments, and for the first year of our success with 'Come and Get These Memories,' we were wearing Marvelette hand-me-downs. I wasn't too proud to beg because they knew more about the business. They were the success story that made me and encouraged me and inspired me to keep going.

"On the road, we didn't get to know them like girlfriends because they had a knack of separating us with two girls in a room and it usually wasn't the group that you sang with. My roommate was Mary Wilson. I got to know her like a girlfriend, like a buddy. The Marvelettes could get all four in a room with a couple of beds pulled in. They could find beds that were accommodatable."

Rosalind Ashford Holmes of the Vandellas adds, "They were nice girls. We were all little teenagers at that time, or just past teenagers. Wanda was a real sweetheart. Wanda, out of all of them, I think she was the sweetheart of the group. Gladys was the one who kept you laughing all of the time.

"Our first trip—when we worked at the Apollo and they took us from Detroit to New York—was with the Marvelettes. I can recall Motown had a station wagon where one of the seats was backwards. Well, the Vandellas had to ride in the backseat backwards all the way to New York with the Marvelettes. At the time, they were a little more [advanced in their career] than us. We didn't mind. It was just the idea, here we are going to New York and then we find out we have to ride backwards all the way. But we all got along. We had a good trip."

In the last half of 1963, the Marvelettes came under the supervision of Smokey Robinson, who long had an admiration for the group's stage act during the Motortown Revue tours. He wrote some songs specifically for the group, beginning with the swinging

"As Long As I Know He's Mine." Gladys assumed the majority of lead, with a high-pitched Wanda coming in on some parts. Here, the narrator is so grateful for her guy's love that she doesn't care about inclement weather or his limited funds. A song highlighted by its catchy "ba-da-loo, ba-da-loo" background chirps, "As Long As I Know He's Mine" was only moderately successful when released in the fall, peaking at number 47 on the *Billboard* pop chart. There was no *Billboard* R&B chart listing at this time. However, "As Long As I Know He's Mine" did spend 16 weeks on the *Cash Box* black contemporary singles chart, peaking at number three. The song was backed with "Little Girl Blue," written by Holland-Dozier-Holland. The background vocals carried the majority of the lead, but featured Gladys singing in a falsetto voice similar to her lead on "You Should Know" from the *Playboy* album. Here, her character, who is in denial, resolves to sit by the phone and wait for a call from a guy who apparently is not faithful.

At this time, Motown experimented with the Marvelettes in an attempt to generate a hit for a nonexistent act. Gladys was paired with the company's in-house backing group, the Andantes, for the single "Too Hurt to Cry, Too Much in Love to Say Goodbye," produced by Brian Holland and Lamont Dozier. Sounding unlike anything previously released by Motown, the song was an attempt to cash in on Phil Spector's successful Wall of Sound formula, as the single sounded like something in the repertoire of the Crystals or the Ronettes. Rather than credit the tune as a Marvelettes' release, Motown chose to issue "Too Hurt to Cry" on the Gordy label under the moniker the Darnells. Deservedly, the song sank without a trace.

Gladys recalls, "Motown didn't come to us and say, 'Girls, would you sign this contract as the Darnells?' It was a trial thing. Berry wanted to see if people would recognize that it was the Marvelettes. That song came out without our knowledge and we had no say-so over that matter. When I heard the recording, I said, 'That's a song we recorded,' and we got a lot of fan mail stating, 'Isn't that Gladys singing "Too Hurt to Cry, Too Much in Love to Say Goodbye?"' When Motown couldn't fool the public with the

Darnells being the Marvelettes, everything stopped with the Darnells; they didn't continue [promoting] the song."

Katherine points out, "When that happened, Motown realized very quickly that the public is much smarter than they anticipated. They noticed, 'These are the Marvelettes. Why are you trying to release them as someone else?' I guess it was done to make all of the money they could. If it's a hit and it goes, then they could put another girl group out there and then they would have two girl groups out there, and one of them originally would've started as the Marvelettes. Then they could get these four or five girls to perform as the Darnells. If the song did well, they would've put out something else, but it would still be under the bogus girl group thing."

Despite a decline in chart success and record sales, the year 1963 was a blissful one for at least two Marvelettes. On August 12, 19-year-old Georgeanna Tillman married 24-year-old Billy Gordon of the Contours, and on December 18, 20-year-old Wanda Young married 23-year-old Bobby Rogers of the Miracles.

A number of Motown's artists and front office personnel were romantically entwined over the years. Rosalind Holmes of the Vandellas points out, "As quiet as it's kept, Motown would liked to have encouraged everybody to hook up with somebody from Motown. It was a thing of keeping it in the family."

Katherine adds, "Many of us would not date anyone outside of the business because another person would not understand the amount of time that you have to spend on the road and rehearsing. Only the people in the business would understand the amount of time you would have to devote to your craft. And not too many guys would understand that. I had a friend who was not in the business, and it became chaotic because the bottom line was that there was nothing you could do with your schedule. They would try to understand but they really couldn't. The majority of the time you would be with [others at Motown] more than you would be with anybody else. You were with the Motown family more than you were with your own family."

During this time, Motown was growing and beginning to reach

mainstream record buyers on a consistent basis. Although the Marvelettes had a solid fan base, Motown did not view them as an act that could be their ticket to a solid position in the pop marketplace. There was perhaps some irony in coming to this

The Marvelettes onstage. Up top, Katherine dances with Ronnie White of the Miracles.
(Katherine Schaffner Collection)

conclusion given how every Marvelettes' A-side reached the pop charts before debuting on the R&B charts. Nevertheless, Motown would view the Marvelettes as a good live act with an occasional hit record.

To push his company to the next level, Gordy looked to the Supremes in general, and lead singer Diana Ross in particular, to pave the way. Even after a long period of failure and watching first the Marvelettes and then Martha and the Vandellas beat then to the top of the charts, the Supremes were regarded as "Berry's girls" from virtually the moment they walked into Motown in the summer of 1960 (they would not be signed to the company until January 1961), and were to be given the big push in 1963. The Motown chairman was immediately drawn to Ross' aggressive pursuit of stardom and the group's overall air of sophistication. Whereas the Marvelettes scored a smash with their first single and were pushed into the limelight without any previous training, the Supremes spent their first three years at Motown in relative anonymity and were allowed to grow as artists. By the time they were given the big push, they had perfected their voices and their stage act. In an effort to get the Supremes on the right path to success, they were paired with the red-hot Holland-Dozier-Holland writing and production team. They gave the group a top 30 hit in the fall of 1963 with "When the Lovelight Starts Shining Through His Eyes." Within a year, the Supremes would become not only the top female act at Motown, but in the world. Gordy would take a personal interest in every aspect of the group's career from the moment they entered the recording studio to the time they left the stage. As a result, other artists at Motown, including the Marvelettes, who were vitally important to the early growth of the company, began to suffer.

Betty Kelly of the Vandellas points out, "The Supremes were easier to work with because they kind of had something, the three of them. I think Berry picked the right group to go into the direction that he wanted to go in. When it was done, I think a lot of people were intimidated or whatever, and instead of continuing to do what they were doing, they let some of it go to their heads and there was envy and jealousy and this and that. I think he picked the right group, but that's my opinion. The writers were writing songs and for some reason they knew which group should have this song and which group should have that song. Holland-Dozier-Holland were geniuses at that. The Marvelettes' songs fit them, and the music that they gave to Martha and the Vandellas fit them."

Katherine states, "It was never a point of us being jealous or envious of any of the other female artists, at least not for myself, because the industry was big enough to accommodate everybody. I think what occurred later on was, Berry and Diana's relationship had a great deal of bearing to a point as to who was going to make it and who wasn't; and not to knock Diana's talent because she is talented in her own right. However, the same amount of energy that was put into [the Supremes] should've been put into everybody.

"Sometimes greed makes you see things differently than they actually are, and it was beginning to be a point of greed. The more you get the more you want to get. Different artists were beginning to hit and you see more and more money coming in. Then the attitude was, 'Well, let's take [the money] and work towards this and let's take it and work towards that. Those that we can do it with, we will, those that we don't want to do it with, we won't.' I've never felt, and I've never seen anything to prove to me differently, that they ever really did that much to promote the Marvelettes at all. I think that it was more that our fan base was so great that Motown had to keep doing different things. We had a *huge* fan base."

She further adds, "As time grew, you did feel slighted, you did feel neglected, you did feel pushed to the curb because everything and everybody had far more importance. It was like, 'Okay, fine, this is what happened. However, you have already outlived your time-span. We've got new up-and-coming artists who are going to bring something totally different to the table. We didn't have to do that much for you at first, but we really don't have to do anything for you now.'

"At the time things were going on, we acknowledged as a group that we were, as time passed on, not treated well. However, you didn't really look at the whole picture. During the time that you're performing and recording and rehearsing, you pay a lot of attention to many of the things that are going on. However, you don't pay *total* attention because there are so many things that are going on, including smoke and mirrors. As time goes on, you begin to rethink things as they occurred."

Martha Reeves adds, "When the Marvelettes were [on top], Motown didn't have the machine that they had after they developed other groups. They learned more about what they were doing to promote, how to expose an act. When Berry finally got somebody who he could depend on and wouldn't turn on him and say, 'I don't want to go there' when he tried to push them, he found [Diana Ross], and she would go where he wanted to put her, and sleep with her, too. That put us on three different levels on his ladder. First, it was the learning group [Marvelettes]; the second group was a commercial asset [Vandellas]; and the third group was the prize that he showed off [Supremes] like you would if you had maybe a German Shepherd … pure bred, of course. There were times when there were [engagements] made for the Supremes that he couldn't have made for the Marvelettes or Martha and the Vandellas."

Ivy Jo Hunter, who would write and produce hits for both the Marvelettes and Martha and the Vandellas, points out, "You can always use more promotion, but it's not just the songs that you go with. With the Supremes, Motown invested money in image. That's where the other girl groups fell behind. They had as good a product, but they were not as recognizable; they were not out front as much and didn't get as much public exposure. You'd hear the records, but you didn't see them every time you opened a magazine or turned on the television."

"All of us female artists seemed to be trying to get the attention of Mr. Gordy," contends Brenda Holloway. "That was their prime mission and goal, more or less the lead singers. The girls that did backgrounds and were not the leads like Gladys, Diana, or Martha, they didn't seem to get involved in that particular aspect of singing. Of course, the lead singers were interested in getting material. We were a group of people, artists that needed material, and so we were always trying to be on Berry's good side so he could give the word to the producers to produce us."

Over the years, there have been reports of a bitter rivalry between Gladys Horton and Diana Ross, particularly on the early Motortown Revue tours. However, Gladys has considerably softened her stance pertaining to Ross and gives her much credit for her superstardom, by stating: "Diana was a leader and I was a leader. We didn't have a lot of fights and arguments, but we did have some that stayed on my mind. I have a lot of respect for Diana. I respect any black woman who is trying to do something and actually does it, because it's hard. People have asked, 'How did you get along with her attitude?' Diana had no attitude. She was just a girl who spoke her mind. The arguments that she and I had were just over kiddie stuff. Diana aspired to be a star; she *knew* she was going to be a star. I had not planned it. It was as if someone threw this career at me. This was the quickest way of getting out of the foster home circuit, and I went for it. Diana Ross was a hustler who always knew what she wanted. She knew she wanted to sing; she knew she wanted to be on Broadway; she knew these things, and she dreamed these things.

"We had some very serious talks because Diana felt like the Marvelettes kept getting hit songs and [the Supremes] were never going to have a hit. She explained to me how the worst material was always played for them, and she had me feeling sorry for her. One time we were doing a show with the Supremes, and she even talked me into letting them star over us. To me, it was nothing but a show, but Mrs. Edwards had gotten angry at me because I had begged her to let Diana star the show, and the Supremes didn't have a hit record out. I tried to make her understand that [Diana] had made me feel sorry for her, telling me all of these sad stories about how this girl and that girl at Motown didn't like her, so I let them star over us ... It was no big deal."

Although it has been widely argued that the rise of the Supremes in 1964 came at the expense of the Marvelettes, this argument is, at best, speculative. The former's ascent to the top happened, perhaps, independently of the Marvelettes experiencing a mini-slump. Most likely, the rise of the Supremes was related to the abrupt departure of Motown's first female superstar, Mary Wells.

Detroit native Mary Esther Wells came to Motown in 1960 as a 17-year-old aspiring songwriter with hopes of getting Berry Gordy to place her tune "Bye Bye Baby" with Jackie Wilson. Having auditioned the song for him at Detroit's 20 Grand Club, the Motown chairman decided to have Wells record the tune herself and signed her to a contract on his new Motown label (the company's previous releases were issued on Tamla). "Bye Bye Baby" would eventually reach number 45 on the *Billboard* pop chart in the winter of 1960–61. A follow-up single, the up-tempo "I Don't Want to Take a Chance," reached the R&B top 10 in the summer of 1961. In 1962, Wells was paired with Smokey Robinson, who, inspired by Harry Belafonte, caught the Caribbean bug and wrote and produced three Latin-flavored singles that Wells took into the *Billboard* pop top 10: "The One Who Really Loves You," "You Beat Me to the Punch," and "Two Lovers."

Wells was now established as the biggest black female artist in the country, and, along with the Miracles, was headlining Motortown Revue tours. Wells' 1963 singles, "Laughing Boy," "Your Old Stand By," and "What's Easy for Two Is So Hard for One," did not do quite as well on the pop chart, although they did reach the R&B top 10. Holland-Dozier-Holland were brought in for "You Lost the Sweetest Boy," which was the flip side of "What's Easy for Two," and became a top 10 R&B hit in its own right in the fall of 1963.

Wells would reach the zenith of her career in the spring of 1964 when she took Robinson's "My Guy" to the top of the *Billboard* pop chart for two weeks in the middle of the Beatles' chart sweep. Wells was at the peak of her career and was idolized by the Beatles, who took her on tour with them. However, the bubble would soon burst. Wells had turned 21 during the run of "My Guy." At the urging of her then-husband, ex-Motown singer Herman Griffin, Wells hired a lawyer and sued Motown, seeking the disaffirmation of her contract upon reaching her 21st birthday on the grounds that she signed it when she was underage. Her wish was granted. Griffin convinced Wells that a $500,000 advance for two years with a two-year option contract with 20th Century-Records was more to her advantage than the 2.7 percent of retail that Motown was paying her in royalties. This proved to be a disastrous career move. Although Wells would generate a few good songs, her 18-year, post-Motown recording career was extremely spotty, and she never came close to matching the lofty heights she enjoyed at Motown. For Berry Gordy, her departure was an embarrassment, although it did not hurt the growing Motown operation as much as if it had come a year earlier. However, he was now in need of a new female superstar to give Motown legitimacy inside the industry, and he looked to Diana Ross to fill that spot. Although the Supremes were "Berry's girls" from virtually the moment they walked into Hitsville, they did not become a priority at Motown until the beginning of 1963; and it wasn't until the end of the year that they scored with "When the Lovelight Starts Shining Through His Eyes." Yet, this triumph was short-lived as their next single, "Run, Run, Run," barely reached the Hot 100.

After the Marvelettes passed on "Where Did Our Love Go," the Supremes recorded it on April 8, 1964. Mary Wells' "My Guy" reached Number One in May 1964, the same month she turned 21 years old and declared herself a free agent. "Where Did Our Love Go" was released on June 17, 1964. In an attempt to get the Supremes additional exposure for their new release, Motown was able to get them added to Dick Clark's *Caravan of Stars* tour, where they were paid virtually nothing. Behind the scenes, Motown had reorganized its national record distribution and solidified its ties with radio program directors. Two months after its release, "Where Did Our Love Go" was the number one pop record in the country, and Diana Ross was on the road to superstardom.

Much has also been made of how the Marvelettes passed up "Where Did Our Love Go" before the Supremes turned it into their first Number One smash; almost to the point of drawing a conclusion that had the Marvelettes recorded the song, they, and not the Supremes, would have enjoyed a string of 12 Number One hits. Actually, the Supremes hated the song as much as the Marvelettes did. However, they did not have the same veto power.

The Marvelettes favored the more upbeat "Too Many Fish in the Sea," which they recorded later in 1964. The flavor of "Where Did Our Love Go" was unlike anything the Marvelettes had previously released as an A-side, both in melody *and* lyrics. At the beginning of 1964, the group's tunes were still aimed at the teenage market and Gladys' slightly raspy, yet adolescent vocal was

After the Marvelettes passed on "Where Did Our Love Go," the Supremes turned it into their first Number One hit and eclipsed all of the other acts at Motown. (clockwise from top) Diana Ross, Florence Ballard, Mary Wilson.
(author's collection)

still carrying the lead on all A-sides. Fans of the Marvelettes were accustomed to an earthy Gladys "telling it like it is" ("Playboy"), or having the upper hand during the end of a relationship ("Strange I Know"), instead of pleading with a boyfriend not to walk out the door. For her character, there was always someone else right around the corner, which explains the Marvelettes favoring the title "Too Many Fish in the Sea" without even hearing the lyrics. Therefore, it is difficult to picture "Where Did Our Love Go" fitting with the Marvelettes, particularly when listening to the finished product of a melancholy Diana Ross purring through the lead while Mary Wilson and Florence Ballard sprinkle "baby, baby ... ooh, baby, baby" throughout the background. In retrospect, Wanda's vocals did add a softer, more mature dimension to the Marvelettes' sound once she began assuming leads in later years, and it is possible to envision her cooing through "Where Did Our Love Go." However, everything she had sung up to that point was relegated to B-side status. Also, given how the Marvelettes were mired in a slump at this time and were no longer viewed as vitally important to Motown as they were, just two years ago, it is doubtful that Berry Gordy would have devoted the same promotional effort behind "Where Did Our Love Go" had the Marvelettes recorded the song instead of the group he now considered to be his top priority.

Gladys recalls, "When they played 'Where Did Our Love Go,' they played 'Too Many Fish in the Sea.' We picked 'Too Many Fish in the Sea' because it had all of the music and the bongos. We were all together and said at the same time we didn't want ['Where Did Our Love Go']. If you listen to 'Too Many Fish in the Sea' without the lyrics, you hear all of the music. When you listen to 'Where Did Our Love Go' without the lyrics, you hear nothing. Diane carried the melody. The melody was not in the music. In 'Too Many Fish in the Sea,' the melody was there. We chose 'Too Many Fish in the Sea' and they gave 'Where Did Our Love Go' to the Supremes, which turned out to be their first big, big, big hit ... It was time for the Supremes to get a hit. They were great singers."

Smokey Robinson again tried his hands with the Marvelettes at the beginning of 1964 with the up-tempo "He's a Good Guy (Yes He Is)." Gladys sang lead on this tune where her boyfriend is the sweetest, most ambitious guy she's ever met. No matter what other people, including her parents, say about him, she will love him through thick and thin. Robinson was unable to weave his magic on the Marvelettes as the teenybopper "He's a Good Guy" only reached number 55 on the *Billboard* pop chart. Clearly, it was time for a change.

The girl group era, which saw its peak in 1963, would encounter a series of events in 1964 that would lead to the beginning of its end. Only two girl groups topped the *Billboard* pop chart in 1964: the Dixie Cups ("Chapel of Love") in June and the Shangri Las ("Leader of the Pack") in November. In 1965, that figure would be reduced to zero. Of course, the Supremes began their run of Number One hits during this time. However, their sound was geared more toward an adult audience.

The primary reason for the demise of the girl group era was the "British invasion," led by the Beatles who, beginning in February 1964 with "I Want to Hold Your Hand," would have six Number One hits that year alone. Ironically, the Beatles, who were staunch Motown fans, covered "Please Mr. Postman" on their 1963 *With the Beatles* LP, as well as hits by other girl groups such as the Shirelles ("Baby It's You" and "Boys") and the Cookies ("Chains"). In addition to heralding a new sound, the Beatles played their own instruments and wrote much of their own material; two factors that created a domino effect in popular music. The techniques of the girl group production teams seemed obsolete; and several writers and producers dropped off the scene, fearing they could not compete with the new sounds. Thus, many of the girl groups that depended on these production teams for their material began to disappear from the charts.

Another factor contributing to the demise of the girl group era was that after three years, the genre had simply run its course, partly due to the market being saturated with second-rate imitators and the public tiring of that sound. In addition to the British

One for all and all for one.
(L–R) Georgeanna, Katherine, Wanda, Gladys.
(Courtesy of Showtime Music Archives)

sound, the girl group era was eclipsed by surf music, folk-rock, blue-eyed soul, and a slicker, more mature Motown sound, the latter of which would help Motown's top three female groups— the Supremes, Martha and the Vandellas, and the Marvelettes— withstand the downfall suffered by their contemporaries at other labels.

CHAPTER 7

The Big Switch

A s the girl group era started to wane, the Marvelettes could no longer hope to find success singing tunes of teenage love and heartache. Their sound would have to take on more of an adult flavor. Although no formal announcement was made, Wanda began singing lead on the group's A-sides as the Marvelettes further distanced themselves from being typecast as a component of the girl group era. Although Wanda's vocal delivery lacked the raw power and emotion that Gladys displayed, she had more of a maturity to her voice, particularly when singing in her natural tone such as on "Forever," as opposed to her earlier falsetto days of "So Long Baby." Katherine points out, "We were growing up and maturing, and I think it would have been a little asinine if we stayed too young. We were growing up and maturing, and many of our fans were doing exactly the same things we were doing; they too were maturing. We were more or less moving with our age group.

"Gladys' voice worked fine for the beginning, but as the music was changing, we needed to change with it."

The Marvelettes were again paired with Smokey Robinson for their first unofficial foray into adulthood. Robinson saw Wanda as something of a "sleeping giant," similar to what he would discover with David Ruffin of the Temptations nearly a year later with "My Girl," and was determined to generate a smash with her singing lead. The result was the joyous "You're My Remedy," released June 8, 1964. A song that featured handclaps and Robinson's customary bouncy production and clever use of lyrics, here Wanda's character does not need medicine, doctors, or nurses when she is sick or needs cheering up; she only needs the presence of the guy to whom she is singing. Unfortunately, "You're My Remedy" would not be the smash that Robinson was looking to score with Wanda singing lead, as the song only reached number 48 on the *Billboard* pop chart. However, "You're My Remedy" was a moderate hit on the *Cash Box* black contemporary singles chart, peaking at number 16. The song also fared better overseas, reaching Number One in Singapore, where it was named record of the year. "You're My Remedy" also reached Number One in the Philippines.

The Marvelettes continued working with other writers and producers. Brian Holland and Lamont Dozier produced the flip side of "You're My Remedy," entitled "A Little Bit of Sympathy, A Little Bit of Love," a song they co-wrote with Tony Hester, who would generate a string of hits in the 1970s for the Dramatics. On

One of the Marvelettes more famous photos as a quartet.
(L–R) Wanda, Gladys, Georgeanna, Katherine.
(Courtesy of Showtime Music Archives)

this moderately paced tune, Gladys uncharacteristically advises another girl to ask for forgiveness should her boyfriend threaten to leave her; the rationale being that it's easier to swallow one's pride than to find a new love.

In the fall of 1964, the Marvelettes released "Too Many Fish in the Sea," the tune they selected over "Where Did Our Love Go." Written by Eddie Holland and Norman Whitfield and produced by the latter, it is regarded as one of the more superior songs to come out of the Motown fold in the 1960s. From its dramatic, bongo-laced introduction, this up-tempo track featured a heavy dosage of tambourines and was anchored by a hip piano line. "Too Many Fish in the Sea" would mark the finale of Gladys singing lead on A-sides. Here, her character tells girls to stop crying over breaking up with a guy and start looking for a better love. The song was further noted for each Marvelette taking a turn singing during the line "Short ones" (Gladys), "tall ones" (Katherine), "fine ones" (Georgeanna), "kind ones" (Wanda). "Too Many Fish in the Sea" was something of a reprieve for the Marvelettes when issued on October 14, 1964, hitting number 25 on the *Billboard* pop chart; their finest showing since "Beechwood 4-5789" nearly three years prior. On the R&B chart it peaked at number 15. The song also did considerably well on the *Cash Box* black contemporary singles chart, hitting number five. Many music critics have dubbed "Too Many Fish in the Sea" a Motown classic and felt that it could have charted even higher had the label put more promotion behind it.

Gladys also sang lead on the B-side of "Too Many Fish in the Sea," entitled "A Need for Love," a song written by Eddie Holland and produced by Brian Holland and Lamont Dozier. On this tune, whereas some people may have a need to cry, to feel important, or to feel tall, here Gladys' character has a need only to be loved.

Shortly after the run of "Too Many Fish in the Sea," Georgeanna was forced to step down. She discovered she had sickle cell anemia and left the Marvelettes on the advice of her doctor. In order to decrease the occurrence of a sickle cell crisis, she needed to avoid strenuous physical activity. In addition, Georgeanna suffered from

systemic lupus, a chronic autoimmune disease where the immune
system becomes hyperactive and attacks normal tissues. Lupus is
a difficult disease to diagnose because it does not typically develop
rapidly; it develops and evolves slowly over time. Because the disease can affect so many organs and mirror so many other mala-
dies, general practitioners, who may not see many lupus patients,
sometimes fail to recognize its symptoms. As a result, some lupus
patients suffer through a long odyssey of treatment before the disease is accurately diagnosed. One of the most common symptoms
of lupus is extreme fatigue; a condition that was further heightened
in Georgeanna due to the poor eating habits and limited sleep
that was a part of the Marvelettes' life on the road. When Georgeanna left the group, she stayed on at Motown as a secretary. Gladys
remembers, "When Georgeanna first started getting sick, she would
just complain a lot. She complained a lot about being tired, so the
doctor finally took her off the road. Georgeanna's always been a
good friend and I was sorry that she had sickle cell anemia that
was causing her to get tired."

Katherine adds, "Georgeanna began to tire quite a lot. I was
aware that she had sickle cell anemia. However, that wasn't until
later, not long after she found out. I was not aware that she had
lupus. It was primarily the doctor's decision for her to stop performing. To live a life on the road is extremely hard. First of all,
you're not able to rest the way you need to and you're not able to
eat the way you should. When we were on the road, there were no
luxury hotels available to you. There were very nice hotels available to you but you could forget about a Radisson or Courtyard
Suite. You primarily stayed in the black community in whatever
city you went into because that's all that was available to you.
Some of them were good, some were not so good. Other times we
stayed in rooming houses and in rooming houses, [the accommo-
dations] weren't so nice.

"For her, [leaving the group] was disappointing because, when
you're out there and you're the age that you are, you enjoyed that
kind of thing. You just kept on pushing and didn't let too many
things get you down. You enjoyed the excitement that came along

with the territory. She may have had issues with [having to step down] because the decision for her to come off the road was not hers. It was in her best interest but it was not necessarily her decision. However, she was married, so it gave her more time to spend with her husband, provided he wasn't traveling. It allowed for a lot more things to occur, more on the normal side of life."

Georgeanna's problems would be further compounded within a year when her husband Billy Gordon was fired from the Contours for his excessive drug use. From the start, her union with Gordon was one that raised some eyebrows at Motown, and not only because of the five-year age difference. The Contours came to the label with something of a reputation for being thugs, and Gordon was considered, by far, to be the wildest of the bunch.

Session guitarist Eddie Willis recalls, "Billy Gordon was a pretty rough character. Before he got started [singing professionally], he was kind of like a thug; a street thug, actually. [The Contours] got lucky, they really got lucky. After they started at Motown, it was only Billy with the wild thing happening. Most of the people around Motown, like some of the studio people, felt that he shouldn't have been going with Georgeanna because he was one of those wild ones. He was a destroyer, really. He didn't care about anybody. He was wild … he was *very* wild.

"Georgeanna was a bit ghetto. She was just down to earth and so regular, really going for it. In the beginning, none of the girls were with this boyfriend thing. It was about trying to build their career. When they started doing gigs with the Contours, that's when they got hooked up with a couple of those guys. It really didn't surprise me when she hooked up with Billy because it was a thing of, okay, Georgeanna's out there in Inkster and Billy was down there in Detroit. The Contours were hot and the Marvelettes were hot; they were really doing their thing. Their thing was, 'Well, we're both in show business. Why not get married whether it lasts or not. Let's do it.' "

Katherine adds, "If you look at today's standards, then Georgeanna would've fit the mold of being a ghetto girl. First of all, Georgeanna was raised by a single parent up until she was a certain age, and her mother may not have necessarily been able to expose her kids to some of the things like … ballet or piano lessons because they had a hard enough time [financially]. Even though things weren't as expensive then as they are now, Georgeanna wasn't exposed to much. It was just a certain kind of way that each [Marvelette], as an individual, was brought up. We were brought up differently, even though we lived in the same area.

"Georgeanna was a very nice, very friendly young lady. We did have our differences and differences of opinion. I've always been a stickler for taking care of business. Georgeanna was happy-go-lucky. Even though she would take care of her business, a lot of times she would be very happy-go-lucky; always smiling, pretty much always laughing.

"Billy Gordon was more or less her type. He was rather wild and he may have brought a certain excitement into her life. He was the only man around besides her stepfather, and maybe she had wanted a male image in her life. Being the oldest child, she would want that male attention and, of course, he was exciting and he was ghetto, so maybe they just clicked."

The Marvelettes were now down to a trio, having lost two members in little more than two years. For Katherine, this was especially disappointing because Wyanetta and Georgeanna were the band mates with whom she went back the furthest. "[Losing] both of them was hurtful because you had been around these people pretty much most of your young teenage years. You laughed, you partied … we were always around each other in one form or another. They stayed on one block, and I stayed on the next block. Wyanetta would oftentimes be at Georgeanna's house and we would be playing cards, laughing and talking, sneaking cigarettes, trying to smoke until we all became big smokers. We spent a lot of time together, so it was like losing good friends."

In addition to losing good friends, Katherine was perhaps most affected by the Marvelettes now having to adapt their choreography to allow for the loss of Georgeanna. She points out, "It took a lot of thought because at the time we came out, basically we had only one microphone [for the background singers]. It was an adjustment of having to change those of us that were in the background and restaging us in that way because those that did drop out came from the background.

"There was a major void [when Georgeanna left]. It's like the biggest adjustment you'll have to make because in some cases you depend upon that other person. It's as if someone's your anchor, and maybe something comes up and it's like, 'I'm not really sure about how this [move] is supposed to be [executed].' Well, you depend on that person who's back there with you in order to do it to enhance your memory of what it should be."

Nevertheless, Gladys, Katherine, and Wanda bonded together to make the group run smoothly. Gladys notes, "After the group had reduced itself from five to three members, we all took on special jobs that made the operation work like teamwork. My job was to make up routines, steps onstage, and choosing songs for each show. Katherine was the group spokesperson. During TV and radio shows, she led the conversation. She was also so good with figures until we made her the group accountant. She kept up with all of our money figures right along with our chaperones. Wanda had become our showstopper. Her good looks attracted many male fans, and she was constantly coming up with new ideas for making our shows unforgettable. She winked at the guys, flirted with the stage guards, and was the sex kitten of the group. Because she loved the clothes, her opinion on dress material was greatly depended on."

The Marvelettes' next single, the straight-ahead "I'll Keep Holding On," was written and produced by Mickey Stevenson and Ivy Jo Hunter. This tune was unusual among Marvelettes' songs because the vocals were recorded in New York instead of Detroit. The Marvelettes were appearing in New York at the time and Stevenson was in such a hurry to get the song recorded that he rented a studio instead of waiting to return to the Motor City. Hunter recalls, "The Marvelettes were working at the Apollo. They dubbed [the vocals] in right there. The track was done in Detroit. New York was the best place to dub them in if they had a release pending soon. Mickey felt strong enough about the tune to go up there and get it done so it would be in the running. Everything had to be at Quality Control at a certain time. It was a situation where they were up for release and all of the producers were recording them at the same time. That was the way it worked most of the time."

"I'll Keep Holding On" was also a bit unusual for the Marvelettes because it had a bass-laden, tambourine-thumping, gospel-flavored arrangement that Stevenson normally reserved for Martha and the Vandellas. Perhaps it was the change of scenery and change in production that led Wanda to deliver one of her most spirited and emotional vocal performances ever on vinyl. On this

By 1965 the Marvelettes were reduced to a trio.
(L–R) Gladys, Wanda, Katherine.
(author's collection)

track, the guy her character is singing to may think he doesn't need love and has no plans for a commitment; however, she will keep pursuing him until he accepts her as his girlfriend. Wanda sings the lyrics in such a testifying manner that as her love grows stronger, you know it is only a foregone conclusion that she will win this cat-and-mouse game. One of the Marvelettes' more underrated fan favorites, "I'll Keep Holding On," was released May 11, 1965, and reached number 11 on the *Billboard* R&B chart while peaking at number 34 on the pop listing.

"Wanda had that little singsong voice," says Hunter. "It wasn't a whole lot of soul in it or anything else, but she had a nice sound and that quality of youth, and that communicates well. It was a nice clean sound; not too much riffing, you just give her a melody and she'd stick with it and you got your song. If you had a good song, she gave you a good performance. Wanda was easy to work with. She was a quick learner and I found her voice to be very commercial. What else could you ask of her? She did a nice performance in the studio and you had no problem recording her. Wanda was a beautiful person."

Wanda also sang lead on the B-side of "I'll Keep Holding On," entitled "No Time for Tears." A down-home-flavored ballad written by Eddie Holland and Norman Whitfield, and produced by the latter, the pair kept the same theme from "Too Many Fish in the Sea." Now that her unfaithful boyfriend has walked out on her, Wanda's character resolves not to cry but to pick up the pieces and move forward with her life. She will find some other guy with whom she can be friends, if not more.

In the summer of 1965, the Marvelettes released "Danger Heartbreak Dead Ahead," a tune that was written by Clarence Paul, Ivy Jo Hunter, and Mickey Stevenson, and produced by Paul and Hunter. An eerie, bass-laden song that started with a piano flourish and featured a tambourine throughout, here Wanda's character schools a girl of the potential pitfalls of giving love and not getting it in return.

Hunter points out, "Sometimes you sit down and you listen to a track and you open your mouth and something comes out and it leads you into the punch line. 'When you give more than you get' ... that's life experience. Some things you just learn out here when you get your head bumped. You look back and you think, 'Boy, what was I thinking about?' "

"Danger Heartbreak Dead Ahead" was issued July 23, 1965, and matched its predecessor by hitting number 11 on the *Billboard* R&B chart. Unfortunately, the tune was a relative disappointment on the pop side, only reaching number 61. Despite achieving only moderate chart success, "Danger Heartbreak Dead Ahead" became an integral part of the Marvelettes' stage show, and replaced "Locking Up My Heart" as the song that ended their set. When they performed the song, the girls held up huge placards that, when lit by black light, flashed the words "Danger Heartbreak Dead Ahead." Katherine recalls, "You really couldn't see the choreography we had for 'Danger' except for the signs because we did it in black light. We were blacked out and all you could really see were the signs. One side of the sign had 'Danger' printed and on the other side 'Heartbreak Dead Ahead' was printed. The signs were black with orange lettering. It was hard at first mastering the cards because you had to flip them in time to the song. We had a *helluva* time learning to master the signs, but once we did, it was very theatrical. We just always came up with something new and different. As I think about it, it's never been done again."

Hunter adds, "I saw their act with the placards once at the 20 Grand. I thought it was clever. The competition out there was kind of stiff and everybody was fighting for something that would make them stand out among the competition.

"At the time the Marvelettes were out there, they surprised me as well as they did on stage. I thought their act was up to par with what was going on at the time. It was the little hand gestures, and the little hip shake, and the nice little steps side to side and spin every now and then. If you saw one female act, you saw all of them. There was not a whole lot of difference between them as far as their routines, but it was their personality. If you were a Marvelettes' fan, then you liked what they did. They were ladylike, they had the wigs and the little short skirts ... They were very cute."

By the time the Marvelettes released "Danger Heartbreak Dead Ahead" in 1965, they were bewigged and artfully made up. (clockwise from top) Katherine, Gladys, Wanda.
(author's collection)

Gladys sang lead on the flip side of "Danger Heartbreak Dead Ahead," entitled "Your Cheating Ways." A tune written and produced by Ivy Jo Hunter and Mickey Stevenson, here her character will not be hurt if the guy to whom she is singing leaves, for he has been untrue before. Ultimately, he will pay for his treatment of her.

At this time, Motown looked to solidify its relationships with England and European record distributors, so in the spring of 1965, Motown implemented a Revue tour of Great Britain, Germany, Holland, and France. The lineup included the Supremes, the Temptations, the Miracles, Martha and the Vandellas, and Stevie

Wonder. The most notable event of this tour was the London TV special, *The Sounds of Motown*, hosted by Dusty Springfield. During the run of "Danger Heartbreak Dead Ahead," the Marvelettes also toured overseas, separate from their label mates, making stops in England, Belgium, and the Netherlands. "When they had the Motown package, we weren't included in that, we went by ourselves," says Katherine. "We went to London and we went to Amsterdam and Belgium. We went there on a promotion type of tour. We were very well-received over there. I loved it. I loved the experience of, first of all, going overseas and meeting the people. When we went to Holland, we had a chance to see the flowers and a real live windmill. Europe has some very interesting spots. We didn't get a chance to travel too much in Europe, but that which we did see was just absolutely beautiful."

A clear indication of the Marvelettes being put on the back burner at Motown during this time was the inconsistency of their album releases. At the beginning of their career, the group cut five albums over a two-year period between 1961 and 1963. However, "Danger Heartbreak Dead Ahead" was the Marvelettes' sixth single issued since the release of their last studio album, *The Marvelous Marvelettes*, at the beginning of 1963. A case can be made that "Too Many Fish in the Sea," "I'll Keep Holding On," and "Danger Heartbreak Dead Ahead" were solid enough to serve as the foundation for a contemporary album, even if the remaining tracks were filler. However, while these three songs fared well on the R&B chart, they were only moderately successful on the pop listings. By now, most of Motown's top acts were consistently hitting the pop top ten, and the barometer at the label had been raised. To Motown, if a song wasn't a hit on the pop chart, it wasn't a hit, period.

Writer/producer Ivy Jo Hunter notes, "The record company had to keep spending money on the artists in order for you to continue to court them. If they're not scheduled for any releases, you have to follow the horse that's going to be in the race. Nothing was happening with the Marvelettes. That was with a lot of people. The primary groups were like the Tempts, the Tops, the Supremes,

Gladys, Wanda, and Katherine in Holland, 1965.
(Katherine Schaffner Collection)

Gladys, Katherine, and Wanda in Holland, 1965.
(Katherine Schaffner Collection)

Marvin [Gaye], the Miracles, Stevie [Wonder], and that's just about it. Their acts were 'established,' for lack of a better word. If you concentrated on them, you really didn't need all of the rest of them, but rather than come right out and tell them: 'We don't need you any more; if you want to go, you can go somewhere else where somebody might be able to put more money into you and do more with you,' they held onto them, and held onto them until their careers kind of dwindled. People like the Spinners, they rejuvenated. Gladys Knight and the Pips, you can't hurt them. The cream rises to the top. The Isley Brothers were an institution before they got to Motown, and since they had music and everything, they were relatively self-contained. Those are the major ones who benefited from their departure from Motown."

In addition to the Marvelettes having to face indifference from the hierarchy at their label, they also had to confront their own internal chaos. Now reduced to the trio, the group was, in many ways, comprised of three separate entities with very little foundation. The small parameters of Inkster, Michigan, may have allowed for Gladys, Katherine, and Wanda to have known of each other as youngsters; however, they were not childhood friends. Katherine and Wanda were never close, despite growing up within two blocks of each other. Gladys, a self-described notorious loner, and Katherine were only casually familiar with each other during their tenure at Inkster High School and did not officially meet until an uninvited Katherine accompanied Georgeanna to Gladys' home for the talent show audition. And it was only at the recommendation of an acquaintance that Gladys asked Wanda to replaced Georgia Dobbins in the group. Prior to this occurrence, they did not personally know each other. Ultimately, this lack of closeness surfaced once the Marvelettes were down to a trio and led to an increase in personality clashes. In addition, with Wanda now beginning to handle all A-sides, her sense of importance in the group escalated.

Katherine explains the situation. "I would say that we were … a combination of being acquaintances and co-workers. In the beginning, we were friends but then the relationship grew into one of being acquaintances. Friends, they don't get jealous of each other and friends can do different things together as well as doing them apart. We didn't have that kind of relationship with each other. We started out as friends but we grew apart to become acquaintances. As we lost different people, each time we lost something. We started out with five, and we had a good mix with the five of us. When we went down to four, we still had a good mix. But when we went down to three, we were dealing with personalities, and personalities were beginning to conflict.

"Wanda more or less became the object of everyone's attention, which is the case with every lead singer. She began to take it to heart. Wanda was short and petite and she was built rather nice and all, and then being the lead singer, it went to her head. She felt that nobody else was supposed to have a boyfriend and nobody else was supposed to get any attention. Gladys was not supposed to have a boyfriend, and I was not supposed to have a boyfriend. She was supposed to be the affection of everyone's eye.

"Gladys was fine with [Wanda singing lead] for awhile, but then Wanda was getting so cocky that Gladys had to come out and defend herself. Wanda was saying that we didn't have any hit records until she started leading, and that was not true. Of course, we had 'Please Mr. Postman' and everything that followed after that until Wanda took over. That was just untrue, and she and Gladys had quite an argument about that.

"That kind of thing causes confusion. I'm not one for confusion. Out there on the road if there was any kind of confusion, I was going to hurry up and bust it up because I'm a no-foolish kind of person. For some of that stuff, it was ridiculous in what they were saying.

"Wanda more or less said that Gladys' contribution didn't mean anything. Needless to say, [Gladys' contribution] did mean a lot. We used to have some heated arguments. One time I got so heated with them, I just blew my stack and on top of that, I had to turn around and get dressed to go onstage and I was *not smiling*. I could not revert back that quickly. I remember Bubba [Knight of the Pips] said, 'I don't know what you were mad about, but you need not ever go back on the stage mad. If any-body knew you, they knew you were mad.' There wasn't too much time between getting upset and me having to appear on stage. I couldn't change like that.

"They would be fighting over different things. Sometimes it would be over a guy or it could be over the music. It could be over any number of things. Within the group, they were the ones where the family feud was going on."

CHAPTER 8

Moving Up

As Motown continued its push into the mainstream, Berry Gordy was not content just to have his artists generate records that sold to the white audiences. He wanted to produce stars that could perform in some of the swankiest nightclubs in the U.S. and abroad. Beginning in 1964, he put his artists through extensive personal refinement classes. Harvey Fuqua was responsible for schooling the acts, aided by his wife Gwen and her sister Anna. However the "school" was not fully instituted until Motown brought in four instructors: Maurice King, and his assistant Johnny Allen, came aboard as the musical director; legendary hoofer Cholly Atkins was hired as staff choreographer; and Maxine Powell was hired to teach etiquette.

Originally from Chicago, Powell was involved in the fine arts from the time she was 14 years old. She took a course in cosmetology under the direction of Madame Walker and studied drama for eight years with aspirations of becoming an actress. Powell visited Detroit for a weekend and was drawn to the city that she saw as something of a slumbering giant. She stayed at the Gotham Hotel near Orchestra Hall and secured a position as a manicurist. Having joined a business and social club and becoming its entertainment director and negotiator, Powell quickly gained a reputation for her class, style, and refinement. She then launched the Maxine Powell Finishing and Modeling School and became a fixture in Detroit's black community. Each year she had a production show that drew anywhere from 1,000 to 1,200 people. She first met the Gordys in the mid-1950s when she hired the family print shop, run by Esther Gordy Edwards and Fuller Gordy, to prepare a unique program for one of her fashion and talent shows. The Gordy Printing Company had a reputation for doing the best work in Detroit. Esther Edwards got involved in organizing the event and got her husband, George, named master of ceremonies. When George Edwards ran for the legislature, Powell supplied office space in a ballroom she owned.

She remembers, "Over a period of years, I guess after three years, Mrs. Edwards' husband, who was the state representative George Edwards, decided to run for a seat on the Detroit City Council. I had an office space vacant and I donated that office space to the campaign. Mrs. Edwards, who had never been a campaign manager before, became her husband's campaign manager, and did an excellent job. The Gordys are a close-knit family, so they all came into the building to help with the campaign, and that's how I met the Gordys.

"I had the Maxine Powell Finishing and Modeling School. Mrs. Gordy saw what I was doing. She took my finishing course, and Esther took it, and Loucye, and then Gwen Gordy, the youngest daughter of the Gordy family, became my model and made the back page of the [Detroit] *Free Press*. The *Free Press* at that time, the back page was a very prestigious space. The African-Americans weren't in the *Free Press* in the '50s unless they committed a crime or did something that was negative."

Despite a limited market in Detroit for African-American models, Powell was able to find jobs for her students. Meanwhile, Berry Gordy had Motown up and running. As Powell became friends with Gwen Gordy, she would often attend local engagements by Motown artists and critique their performances. In 1964, when the expense of operating her ballroom and modeling school was getting out-of-hand, Powell closed up shop and joined Motown full-time.

She recalls, "When Berry was forming Motown and [the artists] were starting to get engagements, whenever one of the artists was appearing someplace, I would go with Gwen. We became friends.

I would watch the artists perform on stage and I'd tell her what they needed to become first-class performers. This went on and on. I'd still run my school and it was successful, where back then there was no market for black models. I ended up getting some of my models to model for Chrysler, Dodge, and Pontiac, commercially. And that wasn't heard of. So, the Gordys knew what I could do. I could get into places, because if you have class and you master your skill, you have to be recognized. That's what I stood for.

"Eventually, Gwen, Mrs. Gordy, and Anna kept after Berry. When something would go wrong, they would say, 'Well, if you had Mrs. Powell, that wouldn't have happened.' They stayed on top of him, and finally he allowed Gwen to hire me. I closed up my shop and went into Motown."

The Artist Development classes were received with varying levels of enthusiasm. However, attendance was mandatory. Whenever the artists weren't performing, they were taken into Motown's studios and taught lessons in self-image, stage presentation, and how to eliminate whatever unsophisticated or unacceptable quirks there were to be worked out. Powell remembers, "Mr. Gordy and I both said, 'You don't have to do any of the things that I suggest to you, none of them. You do have a choice. It's just that you can't stay here. We like you just the same, but you can't stay here.' So they knew from the beginning that if they wanted to grow and develop and be top stars, they had to participate. At the time, some of them thought it was a waste of time; youngsters, you know how they are. Some were from the projects but they were not rowdy or disrespectful, but neither did they have class or were they gracious or did they know anything about being a great, great performer. That's why the finishing school was opened, so they could learn to be beautiful, unique human beings onstage and offstage. First, you have to learn to be who you are and to be great within yourself, so that when you go onstage, all you're doing is being natural.

"I always had high standards. They went to school for two hours every day; not one day, but every day. I had them sit in a circle. I don't believe in anybody sitting behind anyone because everybody is somebody. I wanted them up front. I didn't want them to be shy or whatever their problem was, they were still coming up front. I told them that I was going to open up a department that had nothing to do with singing. I can't even hold a note. I said, 'You're going to be trained to appear in the number one places around the country, and even before kings and queens or at the White House.' Those youngsters looked at me and laughed and said, 'That woman's crazy. All we want is a hit record.' This is 1964. They didn't have the vision at that time. I began to work with each one of them as to what they needed. I started with 'Who are you and what makes you tick?' and I helped them find out what a unique, beautiful flower they were. I gave them stage technique and stage etiquette. This is what I worked with; no bending over, no making faces when you sing, no holding the mike so close to your mouth so it looked like you are going to swallow it. They were taught how to do that and sing pleasantly. They were lifted from being a singer to being a performer."

"I thought [Artist Development] was a good idea," says Katherine, who had to attend class the same day she and the Supremes' road manager Joe Schaffner went to City Hall in May 1965 to get married (Bobby and Wanda Rogers served as witnesses). "You always hoped for something better. Of course, there was no way that you're going to know everything when you're still young and coming up. A lot of the information that you were getting came from people who had been in the business for a long period of time. Motown was growing. As Motown grew and developed, it would have to develop through its artists in order for them to reach a certain plateau. And then times were changing, that some things were not apropos. In order to really move up into the 'big time,' then of course you had to groom your people for the big time. You couldn't take kids off the street and make them into Copacabana stars without doing something first to prepare them. And so, technically, having the Artist Development department part of Motown was only to prepare everybody for better and greater things.

"I did see changes in our appearance and performance as a result of Artist Development. It's just like taking medication. You take it the first day, you don't really feel anything. You take it for maybe four or five days, and you feel a little bit better than you did the first day. You take it until the prescription runs out and you're feeling a helluva lot better and wonder 'what was it that I had?' As time went on, you could see how things began to advance and progress forth for us."

Mrs. Powell remembers, "The Marvelettes were youngsters and they were good singers and they were anxious to learn. I never had a problem with any one of them. We worked with the body language and we worked with word power. It was a pleasure to work with them. Now, some of the artists weren't as easy to work with, but they were one group that was just jolly and happy. I remember saying to the Marvelettes, 'Every time you appear on stage, think of it as a dress rehearsal and do your best. Don't think, "Oh, I knocked them cold last night." Each performance, if you're going to do two performances a night, each one is supposed to be good. People are paying their money.' I tried to think of all the things that would keep them grounded and keep them from going on an ego trip. I wasn't the only one. Berry was doing the same thing and so was Maurice King. Maurice King was a very classy gentleman and so is Cholly Atkins, and so am I. So they were surrounded with class. I'll never forget it. We worked magic with those youngsters.

"I can see them now, 'Have I got this right, Mrs. Powell?' They didn't fight back. I'd say, 'You've got the idea but we just have to work on it more. As long as you are aware that you are making a mistake, half the battle is won. It's difficult to change but you can change because you are a great, unique human being. You can do anything. It just takes time. Some of you may be slower than others but it doesn't matter. You grow and develop on your own time.' The Marvelettes were kids that were not rowdy like some are to-day, or disrespectful. We didn't have that. They were just not polished and they didn't have the know-how and stage presentation. They knew that they were talented, and they loved to sing. They loved what they did."

Martha Reeves adds, "There was a Motown way and Mrs. Powell put us in a mode for society. We had to be accepted. We couldn't go with our gang street ways and succeed, and they knew that. Berry kind of looked at us and saw us as maybe somebody that could be his women, and he wanted us to look that way and act that way."

For the Marvelettes, the Artist Development classes were something of a case of too little too late. With their greatest run of hits coming in Motown's formative years, they often either headlined the early Motown Revue tours or at the very least, had a longer set than most of their contemporaries. As

Sophisticated and soulful.
(L–R) Katherine, Wanda, Gladys.
(Courtesy of Showtime Music Archives)

a result, whatever proper stage technique or etiquette that was missing in their live act, often received the greatest notoriety. This is still something of a sore spot for the Marvelettes, who feel that perhaps Motown was a bit too insensitive in their public criticism of the group.

Katherine points out, "We were primarily the trial and error group because we were the ones who were out there more than any of the others. After a period of time we all were out there quite a bit, and we all moved in different directions.

"The bottom line is that [the Marvelettes] are always going to be the pioneer group. Whether it's acknowledged or not, we're still the pioneer group because no one really came before us.

Whatever errors and mistakes the company made with us, they tried their best not to make those same mistakes and errors with those that followed behind us.

"I have resented through the years different remarks made pertaining to the Marvelettes and us not being able to perform, and of us not even knowing how to go on the stage, etc. When we went on stage, we were 16 and 17 years old and there wasn't a *damn* person at Motown that could give us any real advice on *how* we should be doing it. There was no one to carry us past where they had already taken us. So, yes, you had 16- and 17-year-old kids. You can't expect kids to come out and act as grown ups. You can't expect people to do what you think should have been automatic where there was no one to tell you what you needed to do. Everything was learned through trial and error, and it was learned by watching other artists who had been out there before us. There was really nobody in our own stable of artists who could really tell us that much because it was still very new.

"For statements to be made ... yes, we were green but there was no one there to help us or take us further. Yes, Artist Development was a very good thing for all of us. It helped all of us to perfect our craft. But for these kinds of things to be said ... hell, they didn't know too much more than we did. That's the reason [Motown] had to get professional people who had been in the business at some point in time. These were old jocks. They had been out there for a long time. They're supposed to know more than we know.

"Our ages should have been taken into consideration. There was no one at Motown who could have done anything or would have given us some type of direction because many of them didn't know too much more than we knew. We got a lot of our performing skills from doing record hops. You go and you do your one little record — and you pantomime that — and then you're supposed to be able to get out there and perform live on a stage with a band? It's a whole different ballgame. It was totally unfair, and totally unfair on Motown's part to let something like [public criticism] fly, because they didn't know a damn bit more than we did ... and they were older.

"When we had 'Please Mr. Postman,' no one was prepared for what was going to happen. And I beg to differ anyone who says they were prepared. That's a damn lie. You may have been trying to get ready to be prepared, but you weren't prepared at the time it happened because you were a new upstart company. It may have been a goal of having [a number one record]. However, you were also hoping that you had more time to get it together, and they didn't. For the persona to be that Motown was ready when it happened ... Motown was *not* ready when it happened."

Martha Reeves adds, "The Marvelettes paved the way for Motown's girls; the Supremes, everybody. If they hadn't worked, we wouldn't have worked."

One other sore spot for the Marvelettes and many other Motown artists has been the so-called "Motown myth" that the label signed a bunch of uncouth artists with no manners whatsoever, put them through extensive training, and transformed them into stars who could mix among the upper echelon of society.

"Basically, what it's saying is that we had no culture, we had no upbringing, we had no anything. I beg to differ and it's a damn lie," says Katherine. "That's not true at all. We all had something to bring to the table. [My family] may have stayed in the projects; however, my mom and dad had a whole different outlook for my siblings and me. I was going to dance class and piano classes. I may not have succeeded in promoting it further in my life. However, much of what I had could only be enhanced by what I had already received long before I even knew there was a Motown. If we didn't have anything to bring to the table, then why did you accept us? If you wanted the talent, you had to accept the faults that were with the person."

Rosalind Holmes of the Vandellas adds, "All of us were brought up in families that taught us how to be ladies. I felt I was a lady before I went to Motown, but what I give them credit for was the grooming. I may not have known to walk into a room and sit the proper way in a chair or to use the correct choice of words, but it wasn't like I was a street person. We did go to school and have some kind of training. Our parents brought us up with some kind of training. We weren't … wild. As far as Motown, they groomed us as far as becoming better ladies and knowing how to act in public."

Betty Kelly of the Vandellas continues, "Some of the artists were more street than others and, yes, we learned things from Mrs. Powell, but some of it was already there. Some of them were definitely street and harder to work with than others. In a group, you may have had one or two members that had more finesse than the others. There were some that had a ghetto mentality—they were ghetto—and others that were easier to work with. Overall, I would say there wasn't anyone who came through Motown who had *no* manners. Some were just easier to work with than others."

Mrs. Powell confirms, "I *never* showed a Motown artist how to use a knife or fork or how to send a thank you note to anyone. In the first place, when I came in 1964, Berry was just getting off and running. I didn't go around to see how they were eating."

One change in the Marvelettes' appearance was that, as their sound matured, they were now performing in gowns. It was left to choreographer Cholly Atkins to tone down the group's traditionally high-energy stage act. Originally from Pratt City, Alabama, Atkins (nee Charles Atkinson) began his career in Buffalo, New York, as a singing waiter after he won a Charleston dance contest there. He teamed with William Parton, also a singing waiter, to form a singing and dancing duo, the Rhythm Pals, who played clubs throughout the Northeast in the early 1930s. When that team folded, Atkins landed a job dancing and choreographing acts for the renowned Cotton Club Boys who were appearing with Bill Robinson in *The Hot Mikado* at the World's Fair. In the early 1940s, Atkins teamed with singer/dancer Dottie Saulters and shared stages with such acts as the Mills Brothers, Earl Hines, Louis Armstrong, and the Cab Calloway Revue. In 1946, he teamed with Charles "Honi" Coles and formed the legendary team of Coles and Atkins, which toured with the bands Count Basie, Cab Calloway, Lionel Hampton, Charlie Barnwell, and Billie Eckstine. They worked through the 1950s; but by the end of the decade, tap dancing took a sharp decline. In 1962, Atkins' coaching skills were solicited by the Shaw and William Morris agencies of New York before he took a staff choreographer position at Motown. Atkins had actually begun an on-again-off-again relationship with the label back in 1960 when the Miracles had enlisted his help after the success of "Shop Around." He later worked with the group for the choreography on their 1963 hit, "Mickey's Monkey."

Once Atkins began working with the Marvelettes, the first thing he did was soften their high-energy stage act. He stated, "[Their stage performance] wasn't as professional as it needed to be. It was more like what the boys were doing; that's what most of the girls were doing at that time. It was one of my jobs to get in there and keep them feminine."

Gladys adds, "Cholly was like, 'Bring me your routines and we'll, see how we can work with them.' He was a nice person. He could tap and do a lot of things that the artists could not do. He was a stage presentation guy. He showed you how to put what you had onstage and how to clean up your act, take a bow, how to get on and offstage the right way ..."

Katherine continues, "The main thing with us, the Motown artists were like all diamonds in the rough. We did have our own choreography, but many of us didn't know that much about show business and in order to perfect it and pick out some of the flaws and make it better, Cholly was very good in being able to do that.

"Cholly was very nice. He could be comical at times, but when it came time to rehearse and it was time to learn what you needed to know for the particular song that you were doing, he would very much be about the business. He could be strict. Cholly and I had a bit of a run-in after a period of time because it was like, 'Oh, my goodness gracious. I am doing the absolute very best that I can do,' and he would always seemingly be on my back. It was like ... 'I can't do any better.' So then I got upset with him, and I addressed it. He said, 'Well, Kat, if I get on you and someone else is paying attention, perhaps you've been doing the very best you could, then maybe they would get the idea that they would need to do better themselves.' And I told him, 'Well, you know what, that's all well and good, but I don't like being your whipping person or anyone else's ' ... Oftentimes, you know people well enough to know what you're able to do and who they're able to do it with."

The Artist Development classes prepared Motown's top artists to perform in more upscale clubs. The Supremes would lead the way, beginning on July 29, 1965, with their debut at New York's Copacabana. Practically all of the company's major acts followed the Supremes into the Copa and other clubs of that stature. However, the Marvelettes remained on the so-called "chitlin' circuit."

Rosalind Holmes of the Vandellas notes, "We were always told, 'Well, you know, the Supremes are first.' There was always a thing of 'Well, you're going to be next. We're using the Supremes to open the door for the rest of you girls, and you'll be next.' It just so happened that we got the opportunity to make it to the Copa and it seemed like it just stopped there. None of the other girls ever made it. I don't know if it was timing or what. I know it should've been possible, but all of the groups had a different sound and it could be that [Motown] didn't feel the Marvelettes had the particular sound to be at the Copa, but still they could have been like us. We were taught different types of songs to be performed at the Copa, so it's possible they could've prepared the Marvelettes the same way."

"I was hoping that we would be able to escalate in our career but, of course, everybody is not capable of being able to do that," says Katherine. "If there was anything that they wanted or expected of us, I don't ever recall that anyone ever came to us and said, 'This is the direction of which we'd like to carry you.' Perhaps [Motown] didn't feel they needed to consult with the entire group. They may have thought in terms of consulting only with the lead singers. However, if you are a group, the lead singers cannot make a decision for the whole group."

For the Marvelettes, it was a case of the lead singers making a decision for the entire group. History has painted a picture of Motown pushing the majority of its A-list artists to the next level and leaving the Marvelettes to fall by the wayside. Motown did attempt to upgrade the status of the Marvelettes by encouraging them to do show tunes. However, despite Gordy's prodding, it was actually Gladys who was adamant that the group remain an act that performed primarily in black clubs. She explains, "The Marvelettes were not pushed aside. It's just that we—to be truthful about it—were not better singers. We hadn't been together as long as the Supremes. Even Martha Reeves, who came to Motown after us, and as a secretary, was a great singer. Everybody could sing better than the Marvelettes. We had to work at our harmony. The Supremes could walk in and hit a song right away. Groups that had been together longer than the Marvelettes could sing better than the Marvelettes. It's not that we were pushed aside, it's just that I knew we couldn't do it. What we did on each record was great, but on something like the Andrew Sisters' material and songs like 'Canadian Sunset' that the Supremes could sing, we couldn't do that. We didn't do too much nightclub material unless it was a rock and roll nightclub, and we excelled at that. To do nightclubs, you had to have nightclub material. The Four Tops, the Supremes, the Temptations, they got off into the great harmony. The Marvelettes could not keep up at the time.

"I aspired to theaters the best. The clubs were a little more intimate and people were closer to you, and you had to have club material to be accepted. Everybody didn't have club material, and the Marvelettes have never been a club group; we were a theater group. I aspired more to the Apollo, the Uptown, the Howard, the Regal Theater, and any theater. I think the Marvelettes did a better job there."

Near the end of 1965, Smokey Robinson generated the smash he was looking for with Wanda singing lead on the tune "Don't Mess with Bill." This smooth, mid-tempo glide was the perfect fit for Wanda's breathy, seductive, vocal delivery. Robinson's arrangement of "Don't Mess with Bill" allowed for Wanda to sing the lyrics in a more comfortable, laid-back manner as opposed to the gospel-infused passion she exhibited on her three previous leads. Here, Wanda's character may have cried a thousand times when her boyfriend Bill ran around on her; but whenever he apologizes for his behavior, her love for him increases. She tells other girls to leave him alone and focus their energies on pursuing other men.

"Don't Mess with Bill" was released November 26, 1965, and brought the Marvelettes back to the top 10 for the first time since "Playboy" in 1962. The song reached number three on the *Billboard* R&B chart early in 1966 and peaked at number seven on the pop chart. "Don't Mess with Bill" did equally as well on the *Cash Box* pop and black contemporary singles charts; hitting number nine and three, respectively.

The Marvelettes' career has often been divided into two sections: the early years of Gladys singing lead and the later years of Wanda singing lead. If "Please Mr. Postman," "Playboy," and "Beechwood 4-5789" defined the group during Gladys' tenure as the primary lead singer, "Don't Mess with Bill" would become the Marvelettes' signature tune with Wanda at the helm. The song's chart success also sent a subtle message to the music industry that the Marvelettes could sing adult material. With Wanda's three previous leads — "You're My Remedy," "I'll Keep Holding On," and "Danger Heartbreak Dead Ahead" — achieving less than stellar

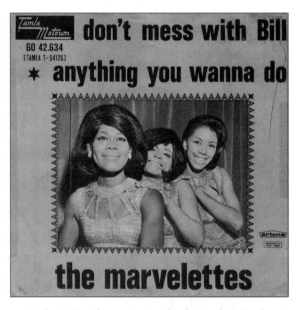

In late 1965 the Marvelettes received a huge shot in the arm with "Don't Mess with Bill." (L–R) Gladys, Wanda, Katherine.
(author's collection)

results on the pop charts, the mainstream audience was not particularly familiar with her voice. Robinson's slick, high-gloss production of "Don't Mess with Bill" gave the Marvelettes a sound that was in stark contrast to anything previously heard on their earlier high-energy singles, and the result was quite appealing to the pop market. With a new sound and a new lead singer being introduced to the pop audience on a grand scale, it almost appeared as if the Marvelettes were a new group. " 'Don't Mess with Bill' was a shot in the arm," contends Katherine. "I felt good about it because we were going through the transition of going from teenagers to young adults. 'Don't Mess with Bill' was an indication of young adulthood; the seriousness of a boy-girl relationship by comparison to a kid type of relationship. Smokey just had the knack for moving us in the direction of where we were to go. He had the ability to get us there."

Ironically, Robinson was initially alone in his opinion of the song's hit potential. Given how the Marvelettes were still typecast in some circles as teenyboppers of the girl group era that had nearly dried up by now, the powers that be at Motown could not foresee them having success with mellow, more mature product. As a result, Robinson had to fight to get "Don't Mess with Bill" released. Ultimately, the musical marriage between Smokey Robinson and Wanda would provide the Marvelettes with their longest run of successful singles since Robert Bateman and Brian Holland produced them in 1961–62. Katherine points out that, "Wanda had the tone for whatever records [Robinson] was doing. If you think in terms of different records that Wanda led that were by Smokey, and if you think in terms of Gladys [singing lead] on those same songs, the outcome would not have been the same. Wanda's voicing and the tone of her voice allowed for it to be good."

During the run of "Don't Mess with Bill," Robert Bernstein (who, as Scott Regen, was a legendary evening deejay at WKNR radio in Detroit) hosted "Motown Mondays," a series of live broadcasts from the Roostertail Club in downtown Detroit. Although the show ran for only six weeks, Motown gave it the full production treatment. The Marvelettes were featured one evening, along with Jr. Walker and the All-Stars, and performed their current hit. Bernstein notes, "I thought their stage act was great. The primary thing that stood out with them was their highly stylized way of singing 'Don't Mess with Bill.' Smokey did a great production on that song. It was too bad they couldn't continue like that. I think Smokey found his female counterpart [in Wanda]. From a production standpoint, he sort of found his female self in the songs he produced for the Marvelettes. Since he himself wasn't a woman and couldn't sing them, he found [the Marvelettes], and it was like a perfect match for his thing, for his feel. 'The Tracks of My Tears,' which was almost the same tempo as 'Don't Mess with Bill,' you can almost hear the Marvelettes in that song. [Smokey and Wanda] were a perfect match."

Motown, at this time, used a highly successful practice of having a hit single serve as the impetus for a greatest hits collection for virtually the label's entire roster. For the Marvelettes, that hit single was "Don't Mess with Bill." *Marvelettes Greatest Hits* was released February 16, 1966, and featured all of the group's previous singles with the exception of "He's a Good Guy (Yes He Is)" and, strangely, "I'll Keep Holding On." *Greatest Hits* was the Marvelettes' most successful LP, reaching number four on the *Billboard* R&B album chart and number 84 on the pop chart.

In the spring of 1966, the Marvelettes followed their smash with the Robinson-penned-and-produced, "You're the One." A midtempo tune that featured an organ and was anchored by a rhythmic drumbeat, here Wanda's character doesn't care if a guy has fancy cars, deep pockets, or dancing ability. Nor does she need trips around the world or other guys. The only guy she needs is the one to whom she is singing. The song was considered to be something of a "Don't Mess with Bill" sound alike, but it lacked the dynamism of its predecessor. "You're the One" was issued April 4, 1966, and reached number 20 on the *Billboard* R&B chart, while peaking at number 48 on the pop listing.

Gladys sang lead on the B-side of "You're the One," a tune entitled "Paper Boy." Here her character is desperate to read the newspaper, for it may contain a story about a guy she left some time ago. She fears he may have found a new woman who treats him better than she did. This, seemingly dated tune, was produced by Smokey Robinson who wrote it with Janie Bradford.

During this time, Motown producers stepped up the custom of using session singers for background vocals on recordings instead of actual group members. The producers had long used additional voices on the recordings of the Marvelettes to make them sound richer and fuller. No one told the Marvelettes until years later. Producers would apply this, not only with the Marvelettes, but also for nearly all of its girl groups. This technique made better use of studio time, relieved background group members from having to rush into the studio when they came off tour, and gave producers the opportunity to get more of the sound they wanted by changing who did background. The background harmonies of the mid-to-late 1960s' recordings of virtually all of the female groups were provided by the Andantes. The practice of using this female trio on background harmonies created a potentially awkward situation for group background singers who may have felt threatened by the former's existence. However, most artists understood the nature of the business.

Katherine states, "I don't know that no longer singing background on recordings bothered me. It boiled down to a point that this was your job, so it was a form of eliminating you from your job. The only time your importance was noticed was when you began to perform out on the stage.

"Fortunately, the young lady who sang the parts that I sang, our tones were very, very close. It wasn't that hard for me to duplicate. Our voice tones were very similar. It wasn't as complicated as it may seem. Our main thing at that point was just learning to perform. We would've liked to have done our own background, but... I think it was a time-saving thing."

Louvain Demps of the Andantes recalls, "All of [the Marvelettes] were sweetie-pies. They were nice girls. When they first came to Motown, the first day they were rehearsing ['Please Mr. Postman'] they asked me how it sounded. I was very proud to be there and for them to ask me how they sounded and how they looked. They were just cute girls and everything, and it was just exciting being with them.

"When they got on that stage, they did good. I remember somebody would say about Katherine, 'Boy, she's like a young stallion out there.' She's tall and pretty and just *did it*. Katherine, with her legs so long; she just looked like she was galloping. All of them looked like they just had so much fun.

"Their sound was not as rounded. I think when they came in they were a little sharp. They were young girls, and we were more polished. When you're in the studio like that, you can hear everything. They were very good onstage, but in the studio you can hear everything. Their harmonies were a little sharp and ours were a little more rounded. Putting them together, they came out nice. We were all in the studio together. What they would do was lower their sound and pull ours up. If it weren't quite like what they wanted, they would pull us up a little more. After awhile, it kind of got so that they put us on there instead of the girls.

"After they really started recording, most of the stuff they did, we were on just about everything. It just happened like that. I don't think anyone started out thinking that we're taking his or her job or anything like that. We were paid to do what we did.

"At the time, you're performing your artistry. You're doing the best for you to do with what God gave you. Sometimes we would do [the Marvelettes] and we would do somebody else. It was just part of what we did. You don't think about hurting anyone. One time when the Tempts didn't want us to sing too much on their stuff, they protested. We didn't have any problem like that with the Tops. Some songs we liked and some we didn't. It was just a job, and we were good."

CHAPTER 9

The Media

More than any other major artist at Motown, the Marvelettes were victims of timing. Their peak years of 1961 and 1962 came before advances were made in the civil rights movement and the whole idea of integration had taken hold. In the mid-1950s, there was still a growing anxiety about the visibility of black performers on television. In this racial climate, corporations, who were particularly afraid of offending viewers in the South, were hesitant to sponsor a program that showcased black talent. Perhaps the most notable casualty of this climate was *The Nat King Cole Show*, which debuted November 5, 1956, on NBC-TV. Cole's variety show achieved favorable ratings, even in the South, but was unable to secure a national sponsor and ended after one season.

During the time when the Marvelettes were topping the charts with "Please Mr. Postman," the only national exposure the group received was an appearance on ABC-TV's *American Bandstand*, following in the footsteps of the Miracles, who in February 1961, was the first Motown act to appear on the show. The Marvelettes made a second appearance on *American Bandstand* in March 1962 to perform "Twistin' Postman." *American Bandstand* was something of an institution, especially with the young. To perform on the show almost assured chart success in the States, and the program was also syndicated to many countries in Europe and Australia. *Bandstand* began in 1952 and was initially headed by Bob Howan. Dick Clark, at the time, was a DJ on Philadelphia radio station WFIL but in 1956, he replaced Howan as *Bandstand*'s host. The show became *American Bandstand* when ABC-TV networked the program in August 1957. In the days of racial segregation, Clark proved to be "color-blind," promoting black artists. He provided his audience with the "best" of pop/rock and roll, not segregated by color as most stations did in those days. Nevertheless, two appearances on *American Bandstand* was the extent of the Marvelettes' national television exposure during their tenure as Motown's number one girl group. "They didn't have a lot of TV then, not on the same level," says Katherine. "Most of the shows we did were local shows for local areas. There weren't that many national TV shows out there. As far as national shows, you had a choice of [*American Bandstand*] and *The Ed Sullivan Show*. Well, we never made it to *Ed Sullivan* because we never got to the more sophisticated kinds of clubs. We did Dick Clark's show just a couple of times."

When the Marvelettes were about to hit a mini-slump in 1963, there were several pivotal events that year that shook the civil rights movement: the freedom cause dramatized in the streets of Birmingham, Alabama, in April and May; the assassination of Medgar Evers in the early morning hours of June 12; the March on Washington on August 28; and the bombing of Birmingham's Sixteenth Street Church on September 15 that killed four little girls. These occurrences brought national media exposure, heightened awareness about racial injustice in America, and culminated in President Lyndon Johnson signing into law the Civil Rights Act of 1964 on July 2, 1964, which banned all forms of racial discrimination in public facilities. The national mandate for public integration increased the need for positive images of black Americans, which Motown's performers provided.

Motown's most immediate beneficiary of the strides made in the civil rights movement were the Supremes. Shortly after the Civil Rights Act was passed, the Supremes had the number one record in the country with "Where Did Our Love Go." Before the year was out, they would top the charts for four weeks with "Baby Love." Three days after the Supremes released their follow-up, "Come See About Me," they performed it, along with their first two Number One hits, at the taping of *The T.A.M.I. Show*, a rock and roll extravaganza that also starred the Rolling Stones, James Brown, the Beach Boys, and others. On December 19, 1964, "Come See About Me" sat atop the charts for a week, then dipped to number three for three weeks while the Beatles' "I Feel Fine" topped the charts. "Come See About Me" then returned to Number One for an additional week. During its interim at number two, the Supremes made their first appearance on *The Ed Sullivan Show* on December 27.

Ed Sullivan was noted for his support of civil rights and had a long-term impact in promoting black entertainers. When the Supremes became the first Motown act to appear on his program, it remained one of the few venues on television that consistently featured black talent. An appearance on Sullivan's program gave artists prime time exposure, and they could expect record sales to triple. Yet, before advances were made in the civil rights movement, none of the black girl groups of the early 1960s appeared on his show, no matter how many hits they had. In time, Motown would incorporate an appearance on *The Ed Sullivan Show* as a final phase of its production line. The company would schedule subsequent appearances by the Supremes and other Motown artists like the Temptations, the Four Tops, Martha and the Vandellas, and the Miracles to coincide with the debut of a new song.

Toward the end of 1964, when the Supremes were making television breakthroughs for Motown, the Marvelettes had recently entered the charts with "Too Many Fish in the Sea." Though music historians have cited this tune as one of Motown's most superior and best remembered, it only got as high as number 25 on the pop charts; not enough of a crossover powerhouse to command an appearance on *The Ed Sullivan Show*.

The Marvelettes did get to perform their current hit, along with "Please Mr. Postman," on a local Detroit teen dance show called *Teen Town* on March 6, 1965. *Teen Town* was the brainchild of Art Servey, Sam Gardner, and the program's host, Robin Seymour. At the time, Seymour was a fixture on Detroit radio, spinning records on WKNR, then the city's number one top 40 station. He had a long relationship with Berry Gordy, dating back to the late 1950s, when the latter was forming Motown.

Seymour recalls, "I met Berry Gordy when he was just starting, when he had Jackie Wilson. One of the big publishing firms in New York came in and said, 'We'd like to start a record company for this guy [Gordy] because we think he's going to be the hottest thing in the world.' So we set up an appointment at the Hotel Statler, which would now be the Hilton. We sat there with Berry and they made their pitch. 'We'll publish your stuff worldwide and we'd like to form a label for you, work out a deal...' and Berry said, 'I'm flattered. Let me give this some thought.' We were going back [to Detroit] together and he looked at me and said, 'Robin, I really want to thank you for this. I'll never forget it, but I think I'm going to start my own label. I just want to take a chance at it. I'll borrow some money from my dad, seven hundred bucks, and I'm going to go in and make some recordings and start a company, but I want to thank you.' It was the beginning of our friendship. I got my TV show with *Teen Town*, which was for about six months or a year, if that. Then I was on the air for close to seven years with *Swingin' Time* and *The Robin Seymour Show* on Saturday night. When I started the show, Motown was starting to make a name... the Marvelettes, Smokey, Marvin Gaye, and the little guy named Stevie Wonder. Every Motown artist that ever recorded appeared on my show first.

"The Marvelettes did my show, did my record hops, and we did shows at the Fox Theater in downtown Detroit every year. I hosted the Motown Revue and then I had my own show called *Swingin' Time* where we used a lot of the same acts. The Marvelettes had a good stage act. It was choreographed well. They tried hard, they did very, very well, and ... if they were with probably any other label, could've gone even further. Psychologically, I think Motown held them back, and it was the same with Martha and the Vandellas. Martha, in spite of everything, got to be, and still is, very big."

Most of the video footage seen on the Marvelettes consists of their performance of "Please Mr. Postman" on this local show.

Seymour points out, "Almost everything that you've seen on any of these old rock and roll shows, especially the black and white stuff, is from us." He further adds, "[*Teen Town*] came in at the time when there weren't 'that many' dance parties. Dick Clark took over at that time and he was huge, and we had *Hullabaloo* that came in later. I was very fortunate. There were two other dance parties that were on the air on Saturdays in Detroit when I started, but after about six months we were the only show in town. So, I won by default. The fact that we were the only one and we had all of the Motown artists ... how could you miss?"

Around this time, other avenues did open up for popular black artists, the most notable being *Shindig*, a prime time rock 'n' roll show that featured live performances (not lip-synced to records) by the top acts in popular music. The show debuted on September 16, 1964, and lasted until January 8, 1966. During this period, virtually all of Motown's top acts were basking in the glow of hit records that reached white audiences. Thus, several of the roster's artists appeared on *Shindig*: the Supremes ("Baby Love," "Come See About Me," "Stop! In the Name of Love,"), the Temptations ("My Girl"), the Four Tops ("Baby I Need Your Loving," "Ask the Lonely," "It's the Same Old Song"), Jr. Walker and the All-Stars ("Shotgun," "Shake and Fingerpop"), Martha and the Vandellas ("Nowhere to Run"), and Marvin Gaye ("How Sweet It Is" "Can I Get a Witness"). Ironically, though the Miracles were hot in 1965 with "Ooo Baby Baby," "The Tracks of My Tears," and "My Girl Has Gone," they performed their 1962–63 hits "You've Really Got a Hold on Me" and "Mickey's Monkey" on the show. It remains a mystery why the Marvelettes never appeared on *Shindig*. During the program's run, they were on the charts with "Too Many Fish in the Sea," "I'll Keep Holding On" and "Danger Heartbreak Dead Ahead." A point can be made that these songs charted well on the R&B listings but did not chart high enough on the pop side to warrant an appearance on the program. However, numerous artists appeared on *Shindig* with less than powerhouse success on the pop charts. It can also be argued that the Marvelettes' early hits, "Please Mr. Postman" and "Playboy" should have been enough for them to meet the program's criteria, particularly since Little Eva appeared on *Shindig* long after her 1962 hit "The Loco-Motion" topped the charts.

Writer/producer Ivy Jo Hunter points out, "They didn't have a whole lot of shows, and the shows that they did have, they wanted your acts that were already hot. If [the Marvelettes] really didn't have the chart thing going on, they were not marketable. If I call you up and I say, 'I want the Supremes on my show' and you're Berry Gordy, you tell me you have another act you want to build. You tell me something like 'I'll give you the Supremes if you take Stevie Wonder, too' or 'I'll give you the Supremes if you come back three months later and take Stevie Wonder.' That was the way they would work it. But they wouldn't use the Supremes to build the Marvelettes."

The Marvelettes released "Don't Mess with Bill" five weeks before *Shindig* went off the air. Given that the song became a top-10 pop hit, it is conceivable that they would have eventually performed it on the show. The group finally caught a break with the arrival of *Hullabaloo*, a youth-oriented rock 'n' roll program in the same vein as *Shindig*, that aired from January 1965 until April 11, 1966 (with reruns continuing until August 29). During *Hullabaloo*'s tenure, the Marvelettes did perform "Don't Mess with Bill" on the show on February 14, 1966.

CHAPTER 10

Adults

T oward the end of 1966, the Marvelettes released "The Hunter Gets Captured By the Game," a masterpiece written and produced by Robinson. Here, Wanda's character tells her boyfriend how she secretly pursued him; learning his habits in order to set a trap to capture his heart. However, her plan backfired. She was so preoccupied with setting a trap for him, she did not realize he was also pursuing her. Before she knew it, she was the one who got caught. Wanda purrs through this tale of "she chased him but he caught her," barely raising her voice above a whisper, while the background vocals are kept to a minimum on this harmonica-laced mid-tempo glide. "The Hunter Gets Captured By the Game" was issued on December 27, 1966, and became an immediate hit, reaching number two on the *Billboard* R&B chart for three weeks early in 1967 and number 13 on the pop chart. "Hunter" also topped the *Cash Box* black contemporary singles chart for a week. Ironically, just as with "Don't Mess with Bill," Smokey Robinson had to fight to get this song released. Motown was still unaccustomed to the Marvelettes singing adult material, and felt "The Hunter Gets Captured By the Game" may have been a little too high-gloss for them.

Katherine asks matter of factly, "Doesn't it seem that it doesn't really make a whole lot of sense? What was going to take 'Hunter's' place? Who had product that would've been better than his product? It doesn't really make a whole lot of sense to me because if he had to fight for its release, who had the next product line, and were they able to release it after that? Since Smokey's product was so successful, were any other writers and producers able to release their product after 'Hunter,' and was it as successful?

"I don't think he had to fight that hard. Smokey was argumentative, so do you really think he would let something slide unless someone else could prove to him that 'Hunter' wouldn't be a hit?

"[Motown] didn't want us to grow up. 'Hunter' was a song that would've moved us into a different realm of music from the doo-wop kind of stuff to the more mellow kind of stuff. We were becoming adults and perhaps Smokey was the only one who could see that we were becoming adults. Not to say that there weren't others, but then again, perhaps he was the one who could see that we were becoming adults and decided to give us adult-type songs. Our fans were becoming adults, too, so we couldn't remain teenyboppers for the rest of our lives.

" 'Hunter' was released in '66. All of us were damn near married and had matured, musically, beyond the teenybopper stage. Thank God, Smokey had enough foresight. He had matured and grown up and he just took us along."

At Motown's Quality Control meetings where decisions were made as to what songs would be released, rarely was a tune selected that was the work of a songwriter who was not a part of the company. In an unusual move, the Marvelettes followed "Hunter" with a remake of "When You're Young and in Love," a song written by Van McCoy that was a moderate hit for Ruby and the Romantics in 1964. James Dean and William Weatherspoon, who a year earlier took Jimmy Ruffin into the pop and R&B top 10 with "What Becomes of the Brokenhearted," produced this thoroughly ravishing track featuring a 15-second drum roll at the beginning and elaborate use of strings and horns throughout. The Marvelettes' version of "When You're Young and in Love" was released April 6, 1967, and reached number nine on the *Billboard* R&B chart, while crossing over to number 23 on the pop listing. The song also became the Marvelettes' only British hit, peaking there at number 13. Despite the chart success of "When You're Young and in Love," this tale of young couples' bliss is often overlooked among the Marvelettes' line of hit songs. For one, its orchestral production was unlike anything previously generated at Motown. Also, this was perhaps the first single credited to the Marvelettes that clearly utilized the Andantes exclusively on background. Nevertheless, Katherine closely identified with the song's lyrics.

She says, "I *love* 'When You're Young and in Love.' In the spring of the year everything, including people, seem to have a love affair going. I don't know if it's the changing of the seasons or what, but everything has a tendency of trying to find more love. Everything, if you watch the butterflies, birds, dogs, any kind of animal is trying to find 'love' or companionship in the spring of the year. Spring is refreshing, it's anew because it's a fresh start after the winter season. When you have spring, you have flowers coming up and blooming, trees spreading out ... I think that it's good because for everybody that was in love, the following spring they're trying to recapture that love that was there. When you look at the way things are, spring, it just gives you a good feeling because everything is changing and blossoming out. As I've gotten older, I can appreciate a song like that because it's introducing something new."

"The Hunter Gets Captured By the Game" and "When You're Young and in Love" were the backbone of the Marvelettes' self-titled LP released March 6, 1967. For the album's cover, each member was dressed in a contemporary day outfit. Ironically, though Wanda and Gladys shared lead on the LP's 12 songs and are given photos of the same size, it is Katherine's photo that is blown up, giving the impression that she is the lead singer. She speculates, "The photographer we had said I had very expressive eyes. I think he was trying to capture something." The album opened with two cover versions: Wanda singing lead on a remake of Robert Parker's 1966 hit "Barefootin' " and Gladys' passionate lead on a cover of Dionne Warwick's 1966 smash "Message to Michael." Both tunes were produced by Brian Holland and Lamont Dozier. Wanda followed with "The Hunter Gets Captured By the Game" and "When You're Young and in Love." As with all of the

*Photo shoot for the Marvelettes' self-titled album, 1967.
(L–R) Gladys, Wanda, Katherine.*
(Katherine Schaffner Collection)

*Photo shoot for the Marvelettes' self-titled album, 1967.
(L–R) Katherine, Wanda, Gladys.*
(Katherine Schaffner Collection)

Marvelettes' previous albums, several producers contributed to this LP's remaining eight songs. Norman Whitfield, who apparently was partial to Gladys singing lead, stepped in for two songs: a remake of "He Was Really Sayin' Somethin'," a tune he co-wrote and produced for the Velvelettes back in 1964; and the mid-tempo charmer, "I Know Better." Smokey Robinson gave them "The Day You Take One [You Have to Take the Other]," which was the popular B-side of "When You're Young and in Love," and a tune the Miracles originally recorded in 1963. On this swingin', bass-laden track that featured chimes and finger snaps, Wanda's character doesn't want any of the bad aspects of a relationship. But then she meets the guy she sings to; now she realizes she must accept that every good comes with some bad. In addition to "When You're Young and in Love," William Weatherspoon gave them "I Need Someone," which featured Gladys on lead. Robert Stouton and Robert Walker produced the symphonic "Tonight Was Made for Love," a tune that epitomized the use of session singers instead of the actual Marvelettes behind Wanda's lead. Stevie Wonder's early mentor and producer Clarence Paul contributed the pleading down-home "When I Need You"; Frank Wilson wrote and produced the heartfelt, mid-tempo "I Can't Turn Around," a tune where Wanda's character is unable to face the reality that a relationship is over; and Harvey Fuqua and Johnny Bristol gave them the up-tempo "Keep Off, No Trespassing," which had Gladys' character telling other girls to stay away from her man. On the latter tune, Bristol says, "Gladys' voice fit the idea of the song. There was a difference in the sound of [Gladys' and Wanda's] voices and knowing there was a way Gladys approached the song as the lead singer; no reflection on Wanda because she's obviously proven to be a great lead singer. Sometimes I can write a song and I can hear a particular person or voice-style of singing. ['Keep Off, No Trespassing'] was one of those situations where Mr. Gordy had given me an assignment on a particular group and there were two or three songs that I did. I just heard Gladys singing that song."

The Marvelettes suffered a huge blow in 1967 when Gladys left the group. She had married Sammy Coleman, ex-trumpeter for Joe Tex, and was expecting her first child. Having been orphaned, she chose to settle down and have a proper home and family life as opposed to trying to balance motherhood with life as an entertainer. Unfortunately, her choice was one that she would almost immediately regret. "Like a fool, I left because I was having a baby," she says. "I needed someone on my side to say, 'Gladys, don't leave this. It's not that easy outside.' Maybe things would've been different for me. I got married and stayed married for maybe a year. I don't even know if I actually got married. The guy who married us wasn't even an ordained preacher. My first child was born with cerebral palsy."

Many critics have downplayed the impact of Gladys leaving the Marvelettes. Given that Wanda was now singing lead on all the A-sides, the change went unnoticed on vinyl. However, the departure of Gladys created a domino effect that caused the group to unravel. At Motown, the Marvelettes were considered Gladys' group no matter who sang lead on A-sides. Once Gladys left, Wanda apparently felt that since she was the primary lead singer, she should now have control of the group. Also at this time, her involvement in drugs was beginning to escalate beyond recreational use.

Katherine recalls the situation, "Gladys worked quite a while [during her pregnancy], and of course she was showing. That wasn't a thing that Motown wanted. It wasn't okay for that time. I asked her if she was going to be coming back after she had the baby. She would have to hire somebody to take care of her son. She said, 'No,' that she would not be coming back. I was really hurt because it seemed like the group was falling apart. When Gladys was there, there was a balance. When she wasn't there, there wasn't one because of the fact that it was me against Wanda.

"Things would've been different had Gladys stayed. Gladys would argue and I wasn't necessarily one that would do too much arguing. When I said something, that's what I said and that would be the end of it, pretty much. Gladys was an arguer and if there were a lot of disagreement from Wanda, then Gladys would argue or debate the point with Wanda. I wasn't like that. I'm not one to argue unless it just gets down to a point where I can't take it anymore. Then I'll debate it until ... I was more or less the peace-maker.

"We always had internal problems but we could work things out. Whatever the problem was we could work it out, through a hollering and screaming session, through a 'sit down and let's talk this out' session, or whatever. Basically, we could work it out. But then that was when Gladys was in the group because there were three people and you could sit down and discuss things. But time went on and things began to change and there was no one in there but Wanda and myself. Wanda began to go off the deep end and that left me to handle everything. And after awhile it just got to be too much because she was just ... *gone.*

"Success went more to Wanda's head. It may have gone to Gladys' head, but she held her composure. Wanda did not hold her composure. Gladys had everything going. She seemed to be more down-to-earth than Wanda. Wanda was the kind who wanted attention. If she didn't get it she would just go about things haphazardly. It was the same thing with drugs. She went about drugs haphazardly. She got involved with coke, she was doing weed ... No one knew about the dangers of drugs. It was just trial and error. I'm not going to pretend to be holier than thou. I had smoked weed as we all have, but then my thing was I didn't want anything to control me, and I knew that if you got some bad shit it would control you. I decided that while I was out there, I made a decision that I didn't want that because there were too many things I had to stay on top of. With me having to stay on top of different things, it was more important for me to take care of business and to stay on top of things than to let [drugs] get the best of me. I cut my weed off after I had smoked it a couple of times because I did not want anything that would con-trol my mind. Wanda did not do that. She began to take anything to get high. The more she got high, the more she wanted to get high. Wanda was a real sweetheart. It's just that drugs and alcohol destroyed her.

"One time when we were working at the 20 Grand, Gladys

Knight and the Pips came through to see us. Before Wanda even spoke to them when they came in to see how we were doing, she asked them for some [cocaine]. I just felt really, really strong about that. Whatever you do, you do it if that is your thing, but still you have to respect other people. I'm a firm believer; you don't let everybody know what you're doing. She asked them that before she even spoke to them, and so then I knew things were going downhill from there."

Unlike the departures of Wyanetta and Georgeanna where the Marvelettes continued on without adding a new member, Katherine and Wanda were now forced to bring in a replacement to fill that third spot. Depending on what was at stake, Motown's hierarchy would take an active role in the personnel changes of its female groups. When Annette Beard left Martha and the Vandellas at the end of 1963 to ensure the health of her unborn baby, Berry Gordy quickly filled her spot with Betty Kelly, then of the Velvelettes. At the time, Martha and the Vandellas were Motown's top female group and were preparing to go out on tour. And, of course, Gordy would be personally involved in every aspect of bringing in Cindy Birdsong to replace Florence Ballard in the Supremes in the spring of 1967. The Marvelettes would not have it as easy. It would appear that Katherine and Wanda would have their pick of the litter of female artists aspiring to be part of a hit singing group. However, Motown did not consider it a priority to fill Gladys' spot. Also, Katherine and Wanda, admittedly, were not proactive in finding a replacement.

After a short hiatus, the Marvelettes brought in Ann Bogan to replace Gladys. A native of Cleveland, Ann had a group, the Challenger III, which recorded for Harvey Fuqua's Tri-Phi label in 1961–62. She also recorded a single with Fuqua, "What Can You Do Now" backed with "Will I Do," in a duo billed as Harvey and Ann. When Fuqua's labels were absorbed into the Motown fold in 1963, Ann became a Motown artist. Prior to joining the Marvelettes, Ann's most notable Motown achievement was singing lead on the Andantes' 1964 release "(Like a) Nightmare," the only Motown single to bear their name as the primary artist.

"It was a couple of months before we found a replacement for Gladys, but it seemed like it took *forever*," says Katherine. "Motown, I think, had no real interest in trying to replace Gladys, which would've made the group disband due to us not having [enough] members. They were too busy grooming their new and rising stars. [The Marvelettes] had done what we were supposed to do, and they really didn't give a damn if we had someone else to replace her or not because we had fulfilled the part of what we were supposed to, and they didn't expect us to make it any further.

"We needed the rest, anyway. All entertainers go through something like that. You're out there but you're making hay while the sun is shining. You keep pushing yourself and pushing yourself. If you don't push yourself, then you'll never make it. [The hiatus] allowed us time to rest and then plan what we were going to do.

"Harvey Fuqua brought Ann to the group and had her audition. But before Ann came, there were no other auditions. When I first heard Ann sing, I just thought that she was hell. Her voice was just so dynamic; she was really bitching as far as being able to really sing and having it completely on the ball. Ann had that gospel voice. I would say that she had a helluva lot of training in church. Usually, people who come from the church, you really can't outsing them. When Ann auditioned, [Wanda and I] liked her."

Shortly after Ann came aboard, the Marvelettes went to Germany for a tour of the Army and Air Force bases. "You always want to lend some moral support to the men and women in the military," says Katherine. "We were told—and I don't know how true it was—that German women didn't care for us as black women. I guess they figured we were trying to move in on their territory."

The first post-Gladys single issued by the Marvelettes was "My Baby Must Be a Magician," again written and produced by Smokey Robinson. The song opens with a guitar slide (also featured at the end of each chorus), courtesy of Robinson's long-time guitarist Marv Tarplin, and a novelty-talking bass intro by Melvin Franklin of the Temptations. Wanda's lead on "Magician" was a bit more emotional in comparison to the group's previous Robinson-produced material; delivered over a bouncy, yet subtle bass-laden

Katherine during some down time at the Army base in Germany, 1967.
(Photo by David L. Jones / Katherine Schaffner Collection)

and conga-laced melody. Singing Robinson's clever metaphors, here Wanda's character praises her boyfriend's ability or "magical touch" to hypnotize her with his eyes and cheer her up with his kisses whenever she's down. A song highlighted by its catchy "presto, chango, alakazam" hook, "My Baby Must Be a Magician" reached number eight on the *Billboard* R&B charts early in 1968, number 17 on its pop listing, and number three on the *Cash Box* black contemporary singles chart. This standout is widely regarded as the Marvelettes' final hit and is one that Robinson reportedly thought would've been a bigger record.

In the spring of 1968, the Marvelettes followed with "Here I Am Baby," again written and produced by Robinson and originally recorded by Barbara McNair a year earlier during her brief tenure at Motown. Wanda is at her sexiest while cooing the title over

Robinson's somewhat funky arrangement. Here, her character is a one-time, fiercely independent woman who had no time or desire for a committed relationship until she surrendered to the guy to whom she is singing. The Marvelettes' version of "Here I Am Baby" peaked at number 14 on the *Billboard* R&B chart and number 44 on the pop listing.

Later that summer, Nick Ashford and Valerie Simpson took a break from their collaboration with Marvin Gaye and Tammi Terrell to write and produce "Destination: Anywhere" for the Marvelettes. The song's melancholy lyrics were in contrast to its spirited, swing-tempoed melody and Wanda's somewhat jubilant falsetto. Here, her character has just been dumped by her boyfriend and she goes to the train station to leave town. When asked where she wants to go, the title is her reply; she is too heartbroken

Wanda at rehearsal at the Army base in Germany, 1967.
(Photo by David L. Jones / Katherine Schaffner Collection)

to care where the train takes her. "Destination: Anywhere" was moderately successful, hitting number 28 on the *Billboard* R&B chart, number 68 on its pop listing, and number 14 on the *Cash Box* black contemporary singles chart.

All three songs were featured on an album, entitled *Sophisticated Soul*, released August 26, 1968. A fourth single was "I'm Gonna Hold on As Long As I Can," produced by Frank Wilson and featuring Ann on lead. This hard-driving, gospel-infused track with a killer drumbeat was unlike anything previously released by the Marvelettes, and it was the perfect vehicle for Ann to show off her chops. On this tune, Ann's frustrated character is unable to move on from a relationship that has ended. Although the guy to whom she is singing no longer loves her, she loves him so strongly that she vows to stay attached for as long as it takes to change his mind. When released at the end of 1968, "I'm Gonna Hold on As Long As I Can" reached the lower portion of *Billboard*'s Top 100 chart at number 76 and missed the R&B chart entirely. Curiously, *Sophisticated Soul* contained "You're the One," the Marvelettes' top 20 R&B hit from nearly three years ago. Wanda sang lead on the album's seven remaining songs. Smokey Robinson gave the Marvelettes a revved-up version of "What's Easy for Two Is So Hard for One," originally a hit for Mary Wells in 1963; and the moderately paced "You're the One for Me Bobby." The "When You're Young and in Love" team of William Weatherspoon and James Dean returned for "Reaching for Something

A new version of the group in the late 1960s. (L–R) Ann, Wanda, Katherine. (Katherine Schaffner Collection)

That I Can't Have," an up-tempo tune sung from the viewpoint of a high society girl in love with a poor boy. He believes he's not the right guy for her, simply because of his empty pockets. Nevertheless, her love for him is so strong that she can't help but continue to pursue him. This tune was released exclusively in the UK in 1969. Weatherspoon and Dean also contributed the lushly produced "Don't Make Hurting Me a Habit." Here, Wanda's character concedes to being unable to leave a guy who keeps breaking her heart. Therefore, she pleads with him to stop hurting her. The rest of the album was strictly filler material. Ivy Jo Hunter produced the Ashford and Simpson–penned "Your Love Can Save Me," which later appeared on the Marvin Gaye and Tammi Terrell 1969 album, *Easy*, reworked as "This Poor Heart of Mine." Hunter also wrote and produced "The Stranger," while the team of Sylvia Moy and Richard Morris—primarily known for their work with Stevie Wonder—contributed the down-home-flavored "Someway, Somehow."

Despite *Sophisticated Soul* containing five singles that charted, the LP only reached number 41 on the *Billboard* R&B album chart, and missed the pop album chart entirely. The Marvelettes by now were used to no longer being a priority at Motown and not receiving adequate promotion for their albums. Yet, the group had always remained etched in the minds of music fans due to their constant touring. Unfortunately, at this time, internal problems heightened, which led to the Marvelettes slipping from public sight as a performing group.

Katherine explains, "Wanda was into drugs. You really couldn't tell her anything. There was the thought that things just were not right and she would fire the girl that dressed us and then I would have to talk to her and get her to come back to the group. The guitar player, she fired him, and I would always have to be the mediator of her firing all of these different people because of the fact that it just wasn't right. Her heavy drinking had a lot to do with it; drinking, getting high. Each thing would have a different response.

"I was tired of the arguments between her and other people;

not necessarily between [her and myself] because she didn't want
to go there. Our wardrobe mistress, her name was Jeanette, and
she was Wanda's sister-in-law. [Wanda] was going through a lot
of changes with [her husband] Bobby, and Jeanette would be
caught in the middle of it, even though she had nothing to do with
their relationship. According to Wanda, it wasn't good, whatever
… She took it out on Jeanette, and it was unfair to take it out on
her when she should've addressed it with her husband. Then
[guitarist] Johnny Gilliam, who was with us through thick and
thin, every couple of days she fired him because of him not doing
something that she wanted. What she wanted didn't have anything
to do with what his job was. I never came in contact with her going
through this ranting kind of thing, but I know it happened because
they came back to tell me how they were going to leave, and I'm
trying to find out why.

"Wanda would be going off, way out into left field, with everybody that was working for us, and I would have to keep it together
and it became entirely too nerve-wracking. After awhile, you didn't
know if she were going to perform or not. There were a couple of
times that we'd get all the way to the gig and she wasn't going to
do the gig. Well, who wants to go through that?! Who wants to go
through the arguing, this, that and the other? I know I didn't. I was
tired. We had to get another young lady to work with us. Wanda
had gotten to the point where she would sing, or she wouldn't
sing. She would go out there more or less to party and wouldn't
give a damn about going out there to sing. We had a contractual
agreement that we had to honor; therefore, we had gotten another
girl that could fill in because we never knew if Wanda was going
to show up or if she wasn't. There had to be somebody there
because Wanda would just go off and she wouldn't show up. You
could have a big argument and then by the time you go out there
[onstage], you go out there with a smile on your face, and that was
getting harder and harder to do. She was a Jekyll and Hyde in the
last years. We had begun to look at another girl to take Wanda's
place; Ann and I were going to sing most of the songs. She didn't
work out because she just didn't have it.

"And poor Ann. Ann didn't know which way to go. Ann was trying to be … Wanda's friend. She knew that Wanda would probably get angry if she didn't follow behind her. I think she thought that if she got in good with Wanda, everything would be alright. However, it wasn't Wanda who determined whether or not Ann kept her job. Basically, the one who determined if she kept her job would've been me. Wanda was at a point where she was out-of-control, so then I would've had the final say-so on whatever went down. That's how we kept the musicians and that's how we kept the girl who worked with us, and our wardrobe mistress. I had to go into several meetings with Wanda but I had to take and bring them into a meeting with me, and we sat down and discussed it. Wanda had hurt many of them in the final days. I was a sounding board and had to tell them, 'Don't leave. I need you …' to give them what they needed in order to stay because basically, I didn't want to be alone with [Wanda]. The thing of it is, we could've hired more musicians, but you don't want to hire different musicians when you don't know who they are. Maybe what would've sounded good to her wouldn't have sounded good to me. So, then, I'd rather keep the people we had instead of bringing in anybody else. On top of that, these people had been with us for years."

In early 1969, Wanda would encounter a personal tragedy that would have a profound effect on her for more than three decades. In the early morning of February 20, a neighborhood friend stopped by the Young home to pick up Wanda's two sisters, Dora and LaMona, to drive them to work. Lurking in the darkness across the street was Dora's estranged husband, who was determined to kill her. When he emerged, he first shot the driver of the car, which prompted Dora and LaMona to run into the house. When LaMona stuck her head out the door to see if he was gone, he shot and killed her, probably thinking she was Dora. LaMona Young was only 18 years old. It has been reported in some circles that LaMona died in Wanda's arms, however it was 12-year-old BeBe Young who cradled her dying sister. At the time of this tragic incident, the Marvelettes were on the road.

To outsiders, it appeared that Wanda's problems with alcohol and drugs began with the sudden and violent death of her younger sister. However, for Wanda's inner circle, LaMona's death only triggered what was already a problematic situation they feel began during the Marvelettes' initial overseas tour in 1965. It remains a mystery what actually happened to Wanda, but it has been speculated that someone spiked her drink.

Bobby Rogers, who at the time was married to Wanda, says, "I think [LaMona's death] had an effect on Wanda, but I think something else happened to her. Sometime when she was in Europe something happened to her. When she came back from [Europe], she was different. A couple of things happened and it was like she had changed. Her friends had become her enemies and her enemies became her friends. She took on a totally different thing.

"Wanda was a nice person; she was really nice. She just got sick along the way... mentally. When somebody does something to you and you don't know it, you think it's you. Usually at a bar when somebody puts something in your drink, you don't know it. That's why unless you leave your drink with someone who you know and trust, when you come back to it, you just don't drink it."

"I would say that 45 percent of Wanda's problems could be attributed to [LaMona's death]," opines her sister BeBe. "I wouldn't say half, because her problems started when [the Marvelettes] came back from overseas. I believed [the spiked drink] is what caused it because when they came back, that's when she started being hospitalized. Then with her drinking and experimenting [with drugs], that just made it worse. I think she started having difficulty in her marriage, then my sister got killed, then with the drinking and experimenting [with drugs], everything just exploded. That's when her drinking really took off; she started drinking really heavily."

CHAPTER 11

The Finale

T ime was beginning to run out on the Marvelettes, but Motown still got an album out on them as part of its fall release in 1969, entitled *In Full Bloom*. The team of James Dean and William Weatherspoon handled the writing and production for much of the LP and kept the flavor light and jubilant, despite some of the songs containing melancholy lyrics. In a clear display of how far the Marvelettes had fallen, when *In Full Bloom* was issued on September 16, 1969, it marked the first time the group released a studio album without the prior benefit of at least one hit single to fuel it. The LP's lead single, "That's How Heartaches Are Made," was issued a week later. The song was previously recorded by several artists, including Patti Labelle and the Bluebelles (1965), Dusty Springfield (1965), and Jeanette "Baby" Washington; the latter scoring a top 10 R&B hit with the tune in the spring of 1963. The Marvelettes' version of "That's How Heartaches are Made" was produced by Clay McMurray, a former promotion man who came to Motown and initially served as something of Norman Whitfield's protégé. Wanda sang lead over McMurray's lush orchestral arrangement, where her character does not heed to her friends' warnings that her boyfriend will treat her badly. Although this apparent womanizer disobeys all of love's rules, she still loves him desperately. A beautiful song, the Marvelettes' version of "That's How Heartaches Are Made" undeservedly sank on the charts; reaching number 97 on the *Billboard* pop listing and missing the R&B chart entirely. The flip side of "Heartaches" was the gloomy "Rainy Mourning," which had Wanda's character unable to shake the rain cloud that hangs over her head since her boyfriend left. Whether she's asleep or awake, she always hears thunder and rain in her heart. Ann Bogan's powerful, gospel-infused voice carried the lead on the funky "Everybody Knows (But You)." The remaining nine songs on *In Full Bloom*, including a remake of the Crystals' 1962 hit "Uptown," were a complete departure from anything previously recorded by the Marvelettes. From the joyous "Seeing Is Believing" and "Sunshine Days" to the angry "Too Many Tears, Too Many Times," the LP primarily served as a vehicle for Wanda to display how she could handle any material that was presented to her.

During the run of *In Full Bloom*, problems within the Marvelettes began to take its toll. The group was no longer touring and Motown was focusing its efforts on Diana Ross' solo career, the newly discovered Jackson Five, and moving its headquarters from Detroit to Los Angeles. Consequently, the company paid little attention to the Marvelettes, and the group soon disbanded without any farewell tour or official announcement. "Things just phased out," claims Katherine. "The internal problems that we had, I had taken them to our management, which was also a subsidiary, and I don't really know if she took it any further than that. Maybe they figured they could handle it themselves, or whatever the case may be. Management was a separate entity; a different avenue than recording. I don't know if our management took it to the head of that department. If she didn't take it to the head, then whenever they had a staff meeting, nobody knew about our internal problems except for the person who was the individual that handled you as an artist.

"I wrote a note more or less asking for help. Basically, I wanted to get it to Berry, and I don't know if it ever did reach him. When there was no help to be gotten, I just figured that our time had come. I would have liked for Motown to take an interest in what was going on, and if they had, I would think that maybe they would have tried to get Wanda some help. We could've gone on and performed, either two girls and a guy, or whatever. But I would've liked for them to try to get Wanda some help in the early stages instead of letting it go on.

"If she could've gotten help at the time, then perhaps she would've been able to have been drawn back into reality for what was going on, but she didn't get help at that time and later in years they tried to get help for her, but then it was too late. When a person has a mental health problem, you need to address that right off the bat rather than let it go on for years and then try to help. Then it's too late.

"I remember visiting her home after a gig; and in just trying to talk to her, there just wasn't any talking to her. When I was sitting down talking to Wanda, she just got up and left the room. I'm figuring that she's going to get something so we can continue on with our conversation. Wanda had gone upstairs and had taken a shower. She came back downstairs and wanted to know who had been smoking a cigar. Well, there was nobody in her house but she and I. So I said, 'Nobody's smoking anything because you're here and I'm here but nobody's smoking a cigar.' But she insisted that someone was, and she talked about people coming in and putting wires around her door where they could listen in on her conversations, and cameras that someone had placed all in her home. That was the last time I went by to see Wanda. When I left her house that day, I knew that she was gone. She had gone so far out the box that I just couldn't handle seeing someone go that far off.

"You would want to continue on but you knew that you could not continue under the circumstances," notes Katherine. "Contrary to popular belief, the final days of the Marvelettes were a bitch, and trying to make it seem like it wasn't would be totally asinine. Wanda was just so out of control and to try to make it seem like it was good … it wasn't good. It was a damn nightmare and I would never, ever want to be in that situation again, and never will."

Katherine went on to a life of fulfillment and contentment outside of show business, and never considered a return to the entertainment industry. She points out, "I never did see the handwriting on the wall that the group was breaking up, but I knew that it was going in a totally different direction and that direction was not good for the group. I would say for maybe the final two years I went into very strong meditation and counseling with the Lord to take and resolve this within myself. I just basically prayed on it, and by praying on it, the Lord released it from me; that it would not be a problem for me, and it hasn't been and it probably won't be.

"That's the reason I can still go out and be a Marvelette and I don't have to perform to be a Marvelette. I can still go out there with a certain amount of dignity and grace and do that and resolve that I don't have to get up there and perform because I already did the performing. I think it's good for the ladies who like to perform but I resolve it within myself that I don't have to perform. It does good to see them but then I often say, 'too bad some of them didn't find the peace that I've found.' Regardless of anything else, I'm still a Marvelette.

"Show business was very good to me. It gave me a lot of things and I was able to travel places I never would've been able to travel to. I was able to meet hundreds of thousands of people who I never would've met, but then there's a time when you have to say to yourself that it's all over now. To leave it like I did was probably the best thing for me because I wouldn't have been able to stand up under that kind of pressure in trying to keep the group together. It wasn't worth it to me because it could have cost me my sanity.

"It was over and I knew it was over. The Lord had prepared me for it to be over, and I knew that whatever happened, He would see me through it."

Ann Bogan went on to sing lead with an RCA trio (with two males) called Love, Peace and Happiness, which itself was part of a larger group, the New Birth, Inc. Her worldly monologue and soulful fervor were the catalyst for Love, Peace and Happiness scoring a minor R&B hit in the summer of 1972 with a cover version of Gladys Knight and the Pips' "I Don't Want to Do Wrong," a tune ironically co-written by Katherine. However, Ann gave up the road to raise her family shortly before New Birth had their breakthrough in 1973 with remakes of Bobby Womack's "I Can Understand It" and Buffy Sainte-Marie's "Until It's Time for You to Go."

The Marvelettes, as a recording and touring entity, may have been nonexistent at the start of the 1970s; however, Motown saw the potential for Wanda as a solo artist; ironic, given her personal problems. "I think they basically were grasping at straws," says Katherine. "The bottom line is that we were a group, and so they were grasping at straws near the end in trying to make it her group. But it wasn't ever going to be her group. There would've been hell raised, big time. There was no way I would've allowed that. They were trying to find something that would work, but first they needed to work on the internal problems, then you can work on everything else. The problems still existed."

Wanda's sense of importance in the Marvelettes may have escalated once she began singing lead on virtually every A-side, yet she never saw the group as a stepping stone to a solo career, nor did she ever push for the group's name to be changed to Wanda Rogers and the Marvelettes. With the group now defunct, Wanda viewed a solo career merely as the next logical step in her profession.

Betty Kelly of the Vandellas opines, "I don't think Wanda ever really considered herself being a big star, or wanting to be a big star. Although she had good looks, I don't think she could've pulled it off by herself. Everybody's not able to do that. Diana did it because it was something that she wanted to do and she had the drive for it. Way back then she was saying that she wanted to be a star. That's exactly what she became.

The Marvelettes near the end of the line. (L–R) Ann, Wanda, Katherine. (author's collection)

People say a lot of things about her but she worked hard. I saw her work. Way back then she was working hard. If you don't have the drive and the talent and the know-how of whatever to get where you need to be, then it won't happen. It never really seemed like Wanda wanted to be a big star or be outside of a group situation."

Smokey Robinson had long wanted to do a solo project with Wanda, and his idea was a collection of older Motown songs that were B-sides or had otherwise been overlooked. Although the album was a solo outing for Wanda, with the Andantes serving as background vocalists, Wanda's name did not have marketing value. To the general public, the Marvelettes did not have an individual identity like the Supremes with Diana Ross or the Vandellas with Martha Reeves. Outside of people in the industry and die-hard fans, few knew that Gladys and later Wanda were the lead singers; they only knew the group as the Marvelettes. Therefore, for marketing purposes, the album was released as *The Return of the Marvelettes* on September 15, 1970. The LP's cover featured Wanda, eight months pregnant, atop a white horse with two women on either side on black horses. Both women—reported to have been Billie Rae Calvin and Brenda Joyce Evans of the Undisputed Truth—are airbrushed beyond recognition in the photograph. Given how the album was to be marketed as a Marvelettes' record, Katherine was asked to take part in the photo shoot for the LP's cover but she declined.

She explains, "They called me and wanted me to do a photo session. Someone called and said, 'Smokey wanted you to do a photo shoot for ...' I told them, 'If I wasn't good enough to sing background on some of the songs, then I'm not good enough to do a photo shoot.' They may have felt that they can get a cleaner sound with the Andantes—and not to take anything away from those ladies because they can sing; they can sing their asses off—but I felt that if I were a part of a group, then you can use me just as well as you could the other girls. So then after awhile I just asked them, 'Why couldn't I sing in the background?' because it would've been a blend of the two voices; the girls who sound like me and me. We would've blended. But, they didn't do that, so therefore, for that reason, I felt the way I felt. Why [use a photo of me] on the album's cover? I don't know if any other record companies did it but Motown used studio background singers. I can understand that if they were blending the girls' voices with our voices, but when they use the girls totally and didn't use us, then what's the point in taking a picture? And how many things on that album did Ann sing on? The bottom line is, no, I just wasn't going to do it. It was just unfair, especially when basically, I was the glue holding the shit together."

The album opened with "So I Can Love You," initially a hit single for the Chicago-based sister trio, the Emotions, in the spring of 1969. Next came "Marionette," which was issued as a single on November 3, 1970, but failed to chart. Here, Wanda's character is singing to a girl who is heartbroken because her boyfriend left her. She had allowed him to control her like a puppet and treat her heart like wood. Wanda's character is almost chastising the girl for having been so foolish to fall for him. Robinson originally wrote "Marionette" with Mickey Stevenson, and the song was intended for Kim Weston, but her version was not released. This was followed by "That's How Heartaches Are Made" from the *In Full Bloom* album. Next came a speeded-up version of "A Breath Taking Guy," a song Robinson wrote for the Supremes in 1963 about a "here today and gone tomorrow" lover. Wanda's version was released as a single on January 11, 1971, but it, too, failed to chart. Following in sequence on the album was Robinson's "No More Tearstained Make Up," originally recorded by Martha and the Vandellas on their 1966 *Watchout!* LP; and a cover of the Crystals' spring 1962 hit, "Uptown." In addition, *Return of the Marvelettes* included covers of three songs initially recorded by the Supremes: a speeded-up version of "Someday We'll Be Together"; their first song, the pleading ballad "After All," which Robinson had produced but had never been released; and the beautiful "Take Me Where You Go," which Robinson had done for the Supremes in 1965. Rounding out the album was "Our Lips Just Seem to Rhyme Everytime," and two songs initially recorded by the Temptations: an up-tempo version of "Fading Away," which was the B-side of their 1966 hit "Get Ready"; and their spring 1964 minor hit "I'll Be in Trouble." *The Return of the Marvelettes,* which took all of two weeks to record, was beautifully arranged and sung wonderfully by Wanda. However, it was released at a time when Motown was still in the process of moving to Los Angeles and ensuring that Diana Ross' solo career got off on the right track. As a result, the LP did not receive preferred status, only getting as high as number 50 on the *Billboard* R&B album chart.

CHAPTER 12

Timeline

The Marvelettes as an entertainment entity was nonexistent in the 1970s as neither Gladys, Katherine, nor Wanda performed in any professional capacity.

Indirectly, the Marvelettes' greatest contribution to Motown in the 1970s came in the form of Gladys Knight and the Pips' hit song "I Don't Want to Do Wrong," which reached number two on the *Billboard* R&B chart and number 17 on the pop chart in the spring of 1971. The song, whose lyrics were about a woman seeking the strength to remain faithful when her man has been away too long, was written primarily by Katherine. However, contributions to the song came from Gladys Knight, fellow Pips Merald "Bubba" Knight and William Guest, and Johnny Bristol (who produced the tune). As a result, in the final analysis, Katherine's songwriting royalty rate was a paltry two percent. She claims, "I did write one time and I vowed after everything went down—the way it went down and I got two percent of the record when basically it was my idea and the whole thing—I would never do it again. 'I Don't Want to Do Wrong' was about *my* life. As far as how the music went, I knew I could hear exactly the way the music should've gone. We were at Gladys' house and we were on the back porch and they had an old piano and we were talking about different things. William of the Pips started playing it and I was giving him ideas about how it was going. We sang and we played around with it and then I just forgot about it until a couple of years later when everybody was on it as a writer, even me, but my percentage was, instead of being 85 percent and sharing the 15 percent with William, then the percentage boiled down to two percent. From that, I was really hurt and I vowed I would never do it again.

"Yes, we were all friends but it's a different thing when money is involved. It doesn't matter to me now because I just learned my lesson. In learning my lesson, everybody has to pay for it because I could be someone who has a lot of hit tunes locked up inside that will never see the light of day."

"['I Don't Want to Do Wrong'] was just a collaboration of writers," says Johnny Bristol. "I don't think it came about any particular way, but we all had some contribution to it: Katherine, Gladys, myself, Bubba, and [Guest]. I'm not in a position one way or the other to say [how much each person contributed]. There are so many writers on the song and there's only so much of a percentage anybody can get. Whatever [Katherine's] contribution was, when I wasn't around, maybe she felt that she had more to do with it. That would be more with her and Gladys [Knight], even though I know they love each other to death."

The group's name did resurface in 1975 when Motown reissued their previous hits on a double-LP as part of its *Anthology* series.

A sad chapter in the Marvelettes' history occurred on January 7, 1980, when Georgeanna Marie Tillman Gordon died at her mother's home in Inkster at age 35 after a long battle with lupus and sickle cell anemia. When Georgeanna's illnesses forced her to leave the Marvelettes in 1965, she stayed with Motown as a secretary for a few years before the company moved to California. Her since dissolved marriage to Billy Gordon produced a son, Darrin. Georgeanna was later employed as a secretary at Plymouth State hospital, and she had attended Wayne State Community College.

Considerable advances have been made during the past ten to twelve years in the diagnosis and treatment of lupus, and early detection and treatment have improved the quality of life as well as the life expectancy of many patients. However, this was not the case in the 1960s and 1970s. Lupus is a disease that is four times more likely to strike blacks than whites, and sufferers are normally young women of childbearing years (Georgeanna was 21 at the time of her initial diagnosis). In addition, blacks are more susceptible to the complications of lupus such as the effects of hypertension. In its advanced stages, lupus can affect the skin and kidneys, blood vessels and joints, the nervous system, heart, and other internal organs. Such was the case with Georgeanna. Gladys remembered that upon visiting Georgeanna in 1977 after briefly moving back to Inkster, she noticed how badly swollen Georgeanna's legs were. At the time of Georgeanna's death, she was suffering from hypertension and peripheral neuropathy, a common neurological disorder resulting from damage to the peripheral nerves. Some of the more common symptoms of this disorder are weakness, numbness, paresthesia (abnormal sensations such as burning, tickling, pricking or tingling), and pain in the arms, hands, legs and/or feet.

In addition to her son (who was 12 at the time), Georgeanna was survived by her mother, Mrs. Annabelle Tillman; three sisters, Sharon, Anna Marie, and Thea; and a stepsister, Ann.

In the spring of 1983, Motown produced a twenty-fifth anniversary television special to celebrate the label's history, complete with a gathering of the artists from Motown's glory years who returned for one night. The show's executive producer, Suzanne dePasse, who was now running Motown Productions, had the daunting task of securing the participation of most of the famous Motown alumni, most of whom were happy to appear. However, Diana Ross, now recording for RCA Records, wanted nothing to do with the show and only reluctantly appeared after word leaked to the press that she would be a "special guest star." In addition, Marvin Gaye appeared only after Berry Gordy himself asked him to, and Michael Jackson initially refused to participate, changing his mind only after Gordy agreed to let him sing "Billie Jean," a song that had nothing to do with Motown. Other one-time Motown artists such as Mabel John, former Temptations David Ruffin and Eddie Kendricks, the Contours, and the Marvelettes were not invited to perform. A case can be made that John's tenure at Motown was relatively short, and the decision to omit Ruffin and Kendricks from the invitee list was an easy one because the current lineup of Temptations was performing that night. One can also argue that the Contours and the Marvelettes were defunct groups. In the case of the Marvelettes, Gladys, Katherine, and Wanda hadn't performed in any professional capacity, either together or apart since 1969–70. All of the Motown acts who appeared that night still performed and, in some instances, occasionally recorded as a means of earning a living. Yes, the Miracles by now had retired and the Supremes had broken up, but their respective former lead singers, Smokey Robinson and Diana Ross, were still contemporary recording artists in 1983. A point can also be made that Wanda may not have been in well enough condition to take to the stage and that Katherine, if asked, may have refused to perform. However, had the Marvelettes appeared on the show, they would not have been prominently featured. Three of the label's top acts from the 1960s, Martha Reeves, Mary Wells, and Jr. Walker, were treated like mere sidebars to the Motown story; reduced to singing brief verses of their biggest hits ("Heat Wave," "My Guy," and "Shotgun") during a medley segment. Had the Marvelettes been asked to perform, they probably would have appeared in this segment, singing a brief passage of "Please Mr. Postman."

Suzanne dePasse did not come to Motown until 1967, by which time the Marvelettes were long removed from their position of importance near the top of Motown's totem pole. And just two years later the group would break up. It is quite conceivable that by 1983 Motown Record Corporation in general, and dePasse in particular, had virtually forgotten about the Marvelettes.

Katherine states, "With *Motown 25* and *Motown 40*, we were just completely ignored. To me it's like building a house on sand, because it will not have a foundation. The foundation will eventually wash away. They refused to admit where we stood and how we stood.

"Even if we didn't perform—which I probably would not have because if anybody asked me to perform, I'm not for it at all—they could've had us as honored guests.

"Later that year or early into the year following *Motown 25*, I had the opportunity to see Marvin [Gaye] and talk with him, and he asked me 'Kat, why weren't y'all at the *Motown 25*?' And I told him, 'Marvin, we were never invited.' He said, 'What do you mean you were never invited?' I said, 'Exactly what I said, 'We were never invited.'" And that's the way it's been with the old Motown, seemingly forever to me. I have no bitterness or anything, but the bottom line is there is a mentality in this country about people who live in the city and people who live in the suburbs. And by us coming from a small black community, which during that time, and even now and then, now, did not have a good reputation, there was no way in hell they were going to give us our accolades. Even today, those who follow a lot of different things pertaining to Motown, they never recognize us, and that is through the pattern of Motown itself."

On February 17, 1987, Georgeanna's estate and Katherine filed a lawsuit against Motown, claiming that "Motown Record Corporation has failed and refused to give true and accurate accountings to the Marvelettes as required under the agreement" and that "Motown Record Corporation was to make periodic accountings of all gross receipts and costs attributable to the sale of records or other recorded media recorded by the Marvelettes, individually and collectively." The suit also charged that "Motown Record Corporation has failed to pay royalties due to the Marvelettes, individually and collectively, as required pursuant to" the agreement that "Motown Record Corporation was to pay royalties to the Marvelettes, individually and collectively." Nearly two years later, almost to the day, a settlement was reached between the parties in which Georgeanna's estate, Katherine, and Wyanetta (who initially was not a participant in the lawsuit) each received a low-end five-figure monetary award for back royalties. Neither Gladys nor Wanda participated in the lawsuit.

Throughout the 1980s, Gladys and Wanda periodically talked of reviving the Marvelettes, but nothing came of it. In the latter part of the decade, Blackpool, England, native Ian Levine, a record producer and a staunch Motown fan, sought to work with all of the old Motown artists. Launching his own label, Nightmare Records, Levine and his partner, Rick Gianatos, sought out every ex-Motown artist who was available.

This project was the first time many of the Motown alumni had seen Wanda since the 1960s, and they were shocked by how far she had fallen. The post-Motown years had not been kind to Wanda. After achieving acclaim and creative fulfillment during her tenure as a Marvelette, she had trouble settling into domestic life. Contrary to some reports, Wanda never did perform as a solo artist around Detroit. She did at times reach out to other labels in hopes of securing a recording contract, but it was to no avail. This led to Wanda continuing her descent into drugs and alcohol. Her marriage to Bobby Rogers ended in the mid-1970s, and she moved from Detroit back to Inkster in 1977. "Wanda hasn't worked since Motown," claims her sister, BeBe. "After *The Return of the Marvelettes*, she didn't sing anymore because she started drinking again. [Adjusting to a regular lifestyle] was very difficult for her. Her marriage broke up and she started drinking. She didn't handle it and was escaping into that bottle."

Former Motown artist Kim Weston, who at times roomed with Wanda on the road and became fairly close to her, was very instrumental in preparing Wanda for the recording sessions. She says, "I was glad that Wanda did [the recording sessions] and I was able to be instrumental in helping her to get herself together. I guess that's because we had been close. They were having problems with her but I took her home with me and we talked. She got it together, she started rehearsing, and she did well ... I thought. I dealt with her like she's a professional, which she was. She's a professional and that's how I treated her."

She further adds, "I went back to Detroit and I went to see Wanda. I was disturbed but ... it takes a toll on you, and I guess it depends on where you are and how you handle it ... What caused her to go that way as far as she did ... I don't know. I feel she needs prayer. That's the only thing that I know that could really help. We all make our own choices. When a person gives up, that still was their choice. I tried to show her love, and in the process she responded. Wanda was very precious, to me. She was very special, she had a good heart, and she laughed a lot. Who knows what would've happened had she not had the kind of spirit that she had."

Publicity photo of Gladys in the early 1990s.
(Courtesy of Gladys Horton)

For the project with Levine and Giantos, Gladys and Wanda recruited Jackie and Regina Holleman, and recorded the album, entitled *Now!*, that was released in 1990. The disc included speeded-up versions of some of the group's biggest hits: "Don't Mess with Bill," "My Baby Must Be a Magician," "Too Many Fish in the Sea," and "When You're Young and in Love." *Now!* also featured five original tunes: "Just in the Nick of Time" and "Holding on with Both Hands," which borrowed heavily from the respective arrangements of Janet Jackson's "When I Think of You" and the Supremes' "My World Is Empty without You"; "Secret Love Affair"; and two songs that Gladys co-wrote with Ian Levine: "Used to Be a Playboy" and "You Bring the Love Into My Life."

Katherine was asked to participate in the project, but declined. She explains, "Ian had promised the Marvelettes and everyone else that they would get a hit if they would record for him. When the artists recorded for him, he had them sign an agreement for x amount of records and he paid them $500 a side. With him paying them that, if the record ever turned into a hit, they would never be able to come back because they signed for $500 a side. Ian wanted me to record and I told him, 'No, absolutely not.' I had learned from the master, Berry. Why was I going to go through the same identical thing with him? If you felt that you didn't get your money from Berry, then you knew you weren't going to get your money after that $500. After it was over, some of the artists came back thinking 'I'm big' … and that wasn't the case at all."

Had Wanda been well enough to continue performing, she and Gladys would have faced another roadblock in the form of Larry Marshak, who owns the rights to the name Marvelettes. A one-time editor of *Rock* magazine, Marshak first got into concert promotion in 1969 by reuniting several former members of the Drifters for revival concerts performed under the Drifters' name. In 1976, he came up with the idea of developing a Marvelettes group, knowing that none of the original members were singing professionally. On December 27, 1976, Marshak filed a trademark on the Marvelettes' name with the incorrect spelling "Marvellettes." Motown had not renewed their ownership of the name they originally trademarked in the early 1960s, leaving the moniker open and available to anyone who wanted to exploit the group's history. Since then, Marshak has fielded several Marvelettes' acts with none of the singers having any lineage back to the original members. His groups perform the original Marvelettes' songs, warming up for major Motown acts and actually work in prominent venues fooling unsuspecting customers. In addition, Marshak has threatened to sue any of the original Marvelettes if they performed. Whereas this threat is of no consequence to either Katherine, who has no desire to sing professionally, or Wanda, who is too ill, Marshak's tactics have proven to be particularly frustrating for Gladys, who still performs.

After leaving the Marvelettes in 1967, Gladys relocated to Los Angeles. She briefly lived in Philadelphia and in Inkster before settling back in Los Angeles in 1984. When the mid-1980s resurgence in the music of oldies acts took hold, Gladys decided to return to the stage. However, she was unsuccessful at recruiting any of her former singing partners to join her. Due to the restraints surrounding Marshak's ownership of the Marvelettes' name, Gladys is unable to simply select two background singers and pass the trio off as the Marvelettes. She has appeared as "G Lady and Good Friends" or as "Gladys Horton and the Marvelettes." Marshak has reportedly offered Gladys a spot with one of his groups, but at a considerably lesser payday than she could obtain on her own. Thus far, she has refused his offer.

She states, "Every time someone called me or spoke to me about [Marshak's] Marvelettes appearing somewhere, the news was like a stabbing. It hurt deeply to know that all of my hard work has been done in vain. And just like a killing, your life, your identity, your hopes and dreams are all slowly being drained away by this type of terrorism.

"Even having a disabled son out of three boys did not seem to bother my imposters. Many of them knew about my misfortune, they just didn't care. Although there were many attacks, I think the big terrorist attack came when I learned that [Marshak's] Marvelettes were appearing at the White House at one of the inauguration balls. Not me, but someone who had nothing to do with the success and the songs I brought into this world, was benefiting from my works. That event may have been one of my greatest moments but I was robbed of it."

Motown has received criticism for not holding onto the Marvelettes' name. The way the trail of events is viewed today, it appeared that Motown set out to intentionally disrespect the Marvelettes by giving up the name and as a result, former lead singer Gladys Horton is unable to perform her past hits on a regular basis. However, this has to be looked at as a case of hindsight being twenty-twenty. As far as Motown knew, Gladys' singing career had ended. Motown either gave up or lost the name at a time when the Marvelettes were a defunct group. Gladys had retired and was no longer singing, and Motown had to have known of Wanda's personal problems. The two people who were singing lead had stopped; therefore, Motown no longer had a need for the name. They only way Motown stood to make money from the Marvelettes was by reissuing their previous hits. Marshak does not make any money from the sale of the original Marvelettes' songs, he only gets paid from live shows. From a business standpoint, if Motown felt that the name still had any value to it, they would have held onto it. Also, if Motown needed to pay off a debt, there was no other name to sell off. At the time, all of the company's notable groups from the 1960s were still performing, with the exception of the Marvelettes and the Contours, and the Marvelettes had the more valuable name. In the 1970s, no one foresaw that there would be a huge nostalgia revival of all of the oldies groups. Critics are also unaware that Marshak has owned the rights to the name since the mid-1970s. It is only prevalent now because Marvelettes' groups have been popping up since the mid-1980s, yet he held onto the name all along. Nothing was being done with it until he was able to take advantage of the nostalgia revival. Gladys is more or less a victim of circumstances.

An awkward situation is created when Marshak's Marvelettes are on tour with other Motown acts from the 1960s who performed with the original Marvelettes and are obviously partial to Gladys' plight. Particularly vocal in their displeasure are Martha Reeves and the Vandellas. Reeves states, "It's a shame to have worked as hard as we have worked to establish ourselves that we could be imitated and it's alright, and it can legally be done and audiences will go to see them and one of our major acts will house them on every show they give and treat the original Marvelettes or the original Martha and the Vandellas the same way he would treat [non-original] Marvelettes. The biggest shame is [Temptations' leader] Otis Williams' camaraderie with some of these people from New York.

"I asked not to work with them, until they cut my work off so bad that I had to bite my knuckles and say I have to eat and not affect my work. When we work, their dressing room is put on the other side of the facility. When I see them, they're coming offstage and we're going on. [Promoters] have the audacity to put us directly behind them. I've been scorned because I don't like them. And it's not because I'm a big bad wolf, but that's an insult to me and it hurts my feelings that it can be done to my friends. These are people who paved the way for me. The Marvelettes were the next big [girl group] after the Shirelles. I'm discovered because of their hit records and now I have to work with some [non-original] people who are taking their money. God knows, Gladys needs the money. She earned it.

"And they do things that Motown would definitely frown upon. They're making it ... *nasty* when we made it beautiful. And that's every [non-original] act I've seen so far who are imitating us. I worked with Gladys a lot and it's such a shame that she's not out there doing her thing because she is such a talented person; very

Gladys in the early 1990s performing "Beechwood 4-5789."
(Courtesy of Frank Johnson)

creative. She thinks and feels show business. She's got a very creative mind and she showed it with the Marvelettes. They had wonderful, *wonderful* routines and they should have been more acclaimed."

"I can appreciate them being a group, but I can't appreciate them going by the name the Marvelettes," adds Rosalind Ashford Holmes of the Vandellas. "When they perform, they'll come out and say, 'This is a hit we made in 19...' If they want to do the Marvelettes' songs, give them some credit. There are people in the audience who grew up with the Marvelettes and actually [the non-originals] are standing there saying, 'This is a song that *we* recorded' and these people know right then and there they didn't record this song. I feel like they should be able to phrase it a different way. As far as them doing the Marvelettes' tunes, that's fine. Everybody does everybody's tunes. I believe it's an honor if somebody thinks you're enough to want to sing your tune, but they should have set that up totally different. I feel like they should not go out and perform and make it sound like they recorded these tunes. That's just misleading the people, and that's like any other [non-original] group.

"As a group, they are good. If you put aside the fact that 'We are the Marvelettes,' if they went out and said ... whatever. The girls can perform. I'll give them credit, they can sing. It's not a thing where I would say, 'Oh, God, they sound terrible.' The girls I have seen perform, I enjoyed their show, but I couldn't look at them as the Marvelettes. I look at them as four girls singing."

Annette Helton continues, "These girls are taking the credit by saying, 'We did this song in the early '60s' and 'We did this song...' They shouldn't do that. We worked with these girls and they should *not* do that. They feel no shame. We work with these girls and it doesn't bother them that they know we're the original Vandellas, that we came from Motown, that we were there at the beginning and all of that. That does not bother them. They don't mind getting up onstage saying, 'Oh, we recorded this song...' They don't mind saying it backstage, they don't even mind saying it around us, and they've never made reference to the fact that,

'Well, you know, that's just part of our act and we know we're not the [original Marvelettes].' They don't do that. They really feel like they're the Marvelettes. It's wonderful that they do the Marvelettes' songs since nobody's out there really singing their stuff. I think it's an honor for somebody to even want to recognize you and continue to keep your name alive. But the Marvelettes were, and people will remember them the way they were. All these girls have to do is call themselves the Marvelettes Revue or the Marvelettes whatever and say, 'This is our tribute to the Marvelettes' but just to take them over ... These girls are too young to be Marvelettes.

"They are nice performers. They get over with their audience. It's just that with us being original Vandellas, it kind of hurts for them to do that in front of us. Somebody could even do the same thing to us, which wouldn't be right. But the girls have nice harmony and sound very nice."

Katherine states, "People would love to see us perform, and that's the reason why these [non-original] groups can do as well as they do. A younger generation of people are looking for their favorite group to be out there singing, and, unknown to them [the non-original Marvelettes] are not a real group. People are hungry for seeing the Marvelettes, and the Marvelettes' name carries a lot of weight. You've got a bunch of girls in their 20s calling themselves the Marvelettes ... All of us are in our 50s. When they say that this is a song they made popular in 1960-whatever ... most of them weren't even born. For them to take and go out there and say that they made something popular ... that's the vulnerability of the public. I can't do anything about it but the other side of it is that all they do is promote our records, and they don't get [royalties]. If they want to perform, fine. I don't want to perform anymore. I've already helped make the name and I don't have to go out there and redo it."

While Katherine obviously does not like the idea of women who had nothing to do with the group's success in the 1960s passing themselves off as the Marvelettes, she does acknowledge that for several years, the Marvelettes were a dormant entity and does credit Marshak for keeping the name alive. She also feels that Gladys should consider swallowing her pride and accept Marshak's offer. She points out, "Larry Marshak is the one who is keeping the Marvelettes' name out there. Gladys feels that she is but it's not true. Gladys has had too many problems trying to perform. My thinking is Larry Marshak is the one with the money. Larry Marshak is also the one who has put threats on her. He's going to have his people out there and he's done a lot of things to stop her from performing, and it stops her from making a decent income. But then again, I don't know what he's willing to pay her. There's a form of greed that comes in because you feel like, 'Why should I be paid $500 when I can go earn $1,500 on my own?' But the other side of it is, with Larry Marshak, you can work more. He's preventing her from working.

"Larry Marshak has been using the Marvelettes' name and Marvelettes' groups for way over 20 years or more. Gladys had no interest [in performing]. When she got married and left the group, she had no interest in returning to the business. Not until we were out of the business every bit of 10 to 20 years, then all of this big urge to go back into it. Well, no, I'm not interested. My final years in the group were *hell*; it was a living hell. She wants me to go back out there?! Why would I want to go back out there?! Why would I want to go back out there when I went through such hell with Wanda, and before Wanda, her?! I have rerouted my life entirely. I was involved with my kids, with my family, and it was more important for me to stay home with my family than to be charging around trying to do everything else. I would have to place that responsibility on somebody else to take care of them or more or less raise them. I wasn't willing to do that.

"[Being in the Marvelettes] was a big portion of my life and a very big portion of who I am. I don't deny that and I do not deny the business. But the other side of it is, I've got a whole different life now and I'm not trying to go back and recapture anything."

The year 1995 saw the Marvelettes receive induction into the Rhythm and Blues Foundation Hall of Fame. At the March 2 award ceremony in Los Angeles, Wyanetta made a rare appearance to take her rightful place among her former singing mates. "They wanted [all original members] and that's the reason she came out," says Katherine. "She was a bit hesitant. She called me and we talked about it and then she considered going." After leaving the Marvelettes, Wyanetta married Larry Motley in 1964 and went to adult education classes to obtain her high school diploma. Today she and her husband are active in their church and in community affairs in Inkster. She states, "I wish I could've sang for a longer time but it was not meant to be. I have no regrets whatsoever. Deep down in my heart I believe it would've been a mistake to rejoin the group. I didn't see it at the time but now I do. I'm saved now; been baptized in *Jesus'* name. I'm singing for *Him* now and I love it! My life is complete!"

The Marvelettes receive their R&B Foundation Hall of Fame awards from Salt-N-Pepa, March 1995. (L–R) Cheryl "Salt" James, Wyanetta, Sandra "Pepa" Denton, Gladys, Katherine, Bobbae Rogers (Wanda's daughter).
(Courtesy of Frank Johnson)

A year later the SMV (Supremes, Marvelettes, Vandellas) Fan Club started a letter-writing campaign in an effort to get the Marvelettes elected into the Rock and Roll Hall of Fame. The captain of this operation was Larry Cotton, a contributing writer for *In the Basement* magazine in England and a die-hard Marvelettes' fan from the very beginning. Through Cotton's efforts, more than 3,000 people worldwide wrote letters to the Hall of Fame recommending the Marvelettes for induction.

He states, "I'm a go-getter and I don't like to lose. When I believe in something, I stand for it. I pushed this thing, and it became international. I got a chance to meet Seymour Stein, the president of the Rock and Roll Hall of Fame. I talked to a popular deejay, Jerry Blavatt, and I got information, and he told me that we had so many letters coming into the Hall of Fame office that it was piled up to the ceiling. There were no other groups with that kind of support. They had to make it if it were done by true votes. Katherine heard about the work I was doing and she got in touch with me and thanked me. I had her on the radio. We had a Marvelettes' campaign special program—we played nothing but Marvelettes' songs. We had people calling in; we were on for three hours, nothing but Marvelettes' music. No one had heard any-

*Brenda Holloway, Gladys, and Claudette Robinson
at the Motown Café in New York City for the taping
of a Motown infomercial, February 1997.*
(Courtesy of Frank Johnson)

thing like it. Then we had it the following week and we started getting more people involved. We got people from overseas involved in it and it got to be a big thing. I interviewed Katherine on the radio many times. It got to be hot and everybody thought they were going to make it. Then Gladys got whiff of it and I got a chance to meet her.

Katherine in New York City, 1997. (Katherine Schaffner Collection)

"I had this going for about three years. Finally, I couldn't afford it any longer. Some of the people worked so hard and they got frustrated and it got to a point where we really weren't getting anywhere, and even if we kept it going, through the politics, it wasn't going to work. I found out there were a lot of people on the Board who just weren't aware of who [the Marvelettes] were. I didn't know what to do. I met Steve Martin and he told me to stop the campaign because it was starting to piss people off. He said he liked the Marvelettes but they just couldn't seem to make the ballot.

"I'm getting ready to start it up again. Now that I'm meeting people who are in the business and who have a little bit of clout. They like what I'm trying to do and think [the Marvelettes] deserve induction. I'm being told now 'Just be patient' and that my time is coming."

Today Katherine Anderson Schaffner, Wyanetta Cowart Motley, and Wanda Young Rogers all reside in Inkster, Michigan. They maintain contact from time to time and occasionally reunite for various tributes and award ceremonies given on their behalf.

Wanda has recently begun making appearances as her health has gradually improved. According to her sister, BeBe, "Wanda's doing well. She's doing different activities and mostly just spending time with the family. When she was living with me [in early 2003], she would go to this program to get a feel of trying to get into the career field. It was like a day program where she would go, work

*Katherine, Wyanetta, and Gladys at the Vocal Group Hall
of Fame Marvelettes exhibit, October 1999.*
(Courtesy of Frances Baugh)

on the computers, and just get a feel for what she wanted to do on a daily basis. She enjoyed that. Then on weekends we go out to the store—she still loves to shop—and that would be about it. She's on the verge of getting her own place. So, Wanda's doing great. As long as she doesn't drink, she'll do great."

In early 2003, Katherine and Wanda attended a tribute at Inkster High School in honor of individuals who graduated from the school and went on to forge successful careers. Darrin Gordon attended the ceremony on behalf of his mother, Georgeanna Tillman Gordon. Katherine notes, "Wanda is always very cordial. I know Wyanetta now more than I did then because she wasn't really out there with us for that long, so … life moves on. I reacquainted myself with Wyanetta within the last couple of years, basically when we went to California to receive the Rhythm and Blues Foundation Award. I had the opportunity to reacquaint myself with her then."

Gladys Horton runs a hair salon with her son in California, and has greatly decreased her performing schedule. Given the problems she's had in the past with Larry Marshak, she is not interested in hitting the stage unless promoters are willing to meet her fee. Gladys is also the most proactive original Marvelette in keeping the lines of communication open with her former group mates. She also stays in touch with Georgia Dobbins Davis, who resides in Westland, Michigan. Katherine states, "Gladys and I are still friends. Many times we can be very civil towards each other and underneath everything, Gladys loves me and I love Gladys. She's a very big part of the reason I had my first job; when you look at it, show business is nothing but a job. I will always have respect for Gladys, and I think she will always have respect for me."

Recognition Day at Inkster High School, January 2003. (rear) Darrin Gordon (Georgeanna's son), unknown man, Norma Taylor. (front) Katherine and Wanda.
(Photo by Manuel Wilson/Katherine Schaffner Collection)

Katherine and Wanda at Inkster High School Recognition Day, January 2003.
(Photo by Manuel Wilson/Katherine Schaffner Collection)

Reflecting on her career as an entertainer, Katherine states, "I think the major thing for me was meeting all of the people and traveling and doing things and realizing how much we as a group meant to so many people, how much they think of you, and how much you're loved by people. You really don't have an idea of how big that is until you're away from it. Every year it seems like it's getting bigger and bigger. To think that we started out in '61, and 40-something years later people think the same thing about us, and then loving us as much as they do, and each generation having their own feelings about us. People just would not realize how many people we have that care about us as a whole. I meet quite a few of them and some of them I never do get a chance to meet but I know their feelings when given the opportunity to meet them, what their feelings are, what they were doing around that time that a song was released. That means a lot.

"When you start out as a kid, you look at how much fun it is. The fun still exists, but then as you get older, you realize even more so that this is your job. Once you begin to look at things as being a job, it ends up being a lot more challenging to deal with and you lose some of the fun of it because the demands on you are so high. But overall, the 'good ol' days' were a lot of fun. Regardless if you get mad, they were a lot of fun. None of our lives would be the same if we had not become the Marvelettes, because we'd be used to the same ol' people, the same ol' faces, the same ol' everything. Being in show business allows you the opportunity to meet people and to share the differences in others, and that right there was absolutely splendid. With that being the case, I'm thankful and grateful that Berry started Motown because it did expose all of us who were a part of the Motown stable to a whole different life and lifestyle, as well as a whole new breed of people.

"Show business is something you can grow up in fast and deal with it and try to learn how to survive and stay alive or you can get caught up in it. Either way it goes, you still end up growing up fast because you have a lot of grown-ups directing your life. When you start out as young as you do, there are a lot of things that you miss in life that people take for granted. It wasn't until my oldest daughter was ready to go to the prom and graduate high school that it really impacted me as to what I missed in my own life. You're performing, you're working, so therefore you're not going to experience going to the prom. You're not going to experience the possibility of walking across the stage with some of your classmates for your graduation. You're not going to find a special dress to have to wear with a special guy to go to the prom. Those are things that you just don't do; you just don't experience them because you're doing your job, which is performing and producing records.

"I did go to my junior prom, but it's not the same. When it came time for my daughters to do their thing for their senior year, financially, I just went way overboard in making sure that they had a memorable senior year, memorable prom, and memorable graduation. I threw both of them graduation parties. I saw to it that they had whatever dress they wanted to have. Thank God I have daughters. What it allowed for me to do was relive, in part, what it could've been or would've been for me had I not been an entertainer.

"I didn't really realize how much a part of life I had missed because of my profession. I enjoyed performing. It allowed for me to meet people all over the world. It allowed for me to visit places that I never would have visited had I not been in show business. It allowed me to do the things that I probably never would've been able to do. It allowed for me to have a fantasy fictitious life."

In the final analysis, the Marvelettes were arguably the top girl group in the country from the latter part of 1961 through the end of 1962. Motown thrived during that period but Berry Gordy wanted more, and no one can fault him for that. When the Marvelettes hit a lull in 1963, Motown looked elsewhere to get to the next level. Gordy knew he would have to pump up the flagging career of the Supremes in order to achieve his goal: to sell records in mass quantities to white America. Ultimately, his plan worked. The Supremes became international superstars on a level achieved by very few black entertainers before or since. Gordy's plan was for them to lead the way for opening doors for his artists to perform in venues that were usually closed to black entertainers. Again, his plan worked. It may have been unfair how the careers of others at Motown were put on the back-burner, but that was Gordy's decision, and it was his company. Every artist at Motown took a backseat at the expense of Diana Ross. Did Berry Gordy have enough resources to put the same energy into the Marvelettes that he put into the Supremes? Only Gordy or anyone with access to Motown's financial records can accurately answer that. Was it fair? Perhaps not, but when a record company attains lofty heights, it loses its family atmosphere. The company doesn't deal in personalities; it's about how many records you can sell. Unlike the Supremes and Vandellas, the Marvelettes were entrenched in the girl-group era. Once that era faded at the end of 1963, adjustments had to be made for them to be perceived as adults. Also, perhaps Gordy did not feel comfortable rolling the dice with the Marvelettes. He had to have known of Wanda's personal problems and he couldn't have been too pleased with the group's camaraderie with the notoriously bad-boy Contours, an act he signed only as a favor to Jackie Wilson.

The Marvelettes may have been third on the totem pole at Motown behind the Supremes and Martha and the Vandellas; however, that position cannot blemish their place in the modern history of popular music. They were dubbed Motown's "quintessential girl group," and in that context they rank near the very top of the list of acts that thrived during the girl group era of 1961 to 1963. The Supremes and the Vandellas must be removed from the pack because their hit records were never aimed at the teenage market. The Marvelettes also wrote two of their biggest hits ("Please Mr. Postman" and "Playboy"), a feat almost unheard of in the early 1960s. If the Shirelles are the barometer by which every girl group of that era is measured, the Marvelettes matched them with ten top-40 pop hits. In addition, these ladies outlasted virtually every act that fit into the girl group mold of the early 1960s. Whereas most groups faltered with the arrival of the British invasion at the beginning of 1964, the Marvelettes continued to hold a consistent presence on the charts for the remainder of the decade, churning out such post-girl group era classics as "Too Many Fish in the Sea," "Don't Mess with Bill," and "The Hunter Gets Captured By the Game." They were the first female act with a million-seller at Motown, they reigned in the early 1960s as one of the biggest groups in the country, and they helped open the door for Motown to become the biggest black-owned record company in the world. The pride of tiny Inkster, Michigan, the Marvelettes were high-energy, they were dynamic, they were cute, they were sexy, and they were honest, down-to-earth homegirls. That's why they were so beloved and why they built a massive following that continues to this day.

CHAPTER 13

Author's Note

first became aware of the Marvelettes sometime between ages two and three when I fell in love with their then-current single "My Baby Must Be a Magician." After the song had run its course, I had all but forgotten about the group until I got my hands on *The Motown Story: The First Decade*, released in 1973. This was a five-volume set of Motown's greatest hits from the 1960s and featured live, in-person interviews with the artists who recorded them. I was then introduced to the songs "Please Mr. Postman" and "Playboy" and the names Gladys Horton, Wanda Rogers, and Katherine Anderson; the latter who gave the interview for the two Marvelettes' songs included in that set.

Throughout the 1980s, I became aware of some of the group's other hits, notably "Don't Mess with Bill," "The Hunter Gets Captured By the Game," and "Beechwood 4-5789," from listening to various oldies stations. The 1980s also saw a renewed interest in Motown's golden era of the 1960s. During the latter part of the decade, several books on Motown Record Corporation and its artists began hitting the shelves. Many of these books were written by the artists themselves, beginning with Mary Wilson's *Dreamgirl: My Life As a Supreme* in 1986. However, the Marvelettes at this time were all but forgotten. They were excluded from Motown's 25th anniversary television special in 1983, and only industry insiders had any idea what became of them. It wasn't until 1989 when Raynoma Gordy Singleton released *Berry and Me* that there was any public information about Wanda Young Rogers, sadly, falling on hard times. Gradually, throughout the early part of the 1990s, I learned that Katherine Anderson Schaffner retired from the music industry after the Marvelettes broke up in 1969, and was living in Michigan. Information about Gladys Horton and Wanda Rogers was a bit murky because press releases on performances by the non-original Marvelettes erroneously stated "Gladys Horton and Wanda Rogers occasionally make guest appearances."

In J. Randy Taraborrelli's book, *Motown: Hot Wax, Cool City & Solid Gold*, I read a quote by Katherine stating how her kids asked her about her gold records from Motown and that her response was, "There are none." That passage stayed with me and actually became the impetus for my first two books: *A Touch of Classic Soul: Soul Singers of the Early 1970s* (1996) and *A Touch of Classic Soul 2: The Late 1970s* (2001). Somewhere around 1997–98, I decided that I wanted to write a book about the Marvelettes. I had been a fan of Motown's music since day one and considered it "my right" to pen a tome about one of the label's major acts that thus far had not had a book written on them. I didn't know where to start, but while I was preoccupied with the aforementioned two books, subconsciously I gradually began collecting their music and whatever written information was available. Ideally, I would've liked to have had the participation of Wanda Young Rogers, simply because she sang lead on my three favorite Marvelettes' songs: "Don't Mess with Bill," "The Hunter Gets Captured By the Game," and "My Baby Must Be a Magician." However, I knew she was too ill to take part in something as in-depth as the composition of a book. I also noticed that whenever there was a story written on the Marvelettes, it was usually the media-friendly Katherine who was quoted. Gladys simply remained a mystery. The only information available on her was that she still performed but could not use the Marvelettes' name because someone else owned the rights to it.

When I was actually ready to get started, I figured I would go through an entertainment editor in Detroit who could perhaps put me in touch with Katherine, namely Susan Whithall, who interviewed Katherine for the book, *Women of Motown*.

I caught a break one Saturday night in the spring of 2001 when

I was at an oldies gig selling my first two books and met Frances Baugh, the Marvelettes' fan club president. She told me Gladys Horton had written a manuscript about the Marvelettes and asked if I would be interested in publishing it. *Of course* I would. I had heard reports of Gladys being wary of the media and didn't quite know what to expect when I called her two days later. However, I found her to be quite personable and *extremely* open about some of the scuttlebutt that went on at Motown during the 1960s.

I sent Gladys a copy of my books so she could judge for herself what kind of writer I am. We spoke a week later and she suggested that rather than tighten up her manuscript (which as of this writing I have not seen), I should write a book with input from all of the living Marvelettes, and from the family of the late Georgeanna Tillman Gordon. Gladys then gave me the addresses of her former singing partners, along with contact information for Georgia Dobbins, who dropped out of the group before their first recording, and two teachers from Inkster High School. Due to something of a conflict of interest with her own manuscript, Gladys decided that her participation for this project would be limited. A few weeks later I got a call from Katherine. Once assured that this book would be an original project and not an adjustment to Gladys' manuscript, she agreed to participate. I never heard from the families of Wanda or Georgeanna, and realized that Wyanetta's input would be minimal due to her limited tenure in the group.

Early on, I realized that I had my work cut out for me. Of the five original Marvelettes, one is deceased (Georgeanna), one is ill (Wanda), one left the group almost immediately (Wyanetta), and one chose to offer limited participation (Gladys). In a roundabout way, it got back to my original plan at the start of the millennium that input on a book about the Marvelettes would come primarily from Katherine.

Almost immediately, I knew I had a challenge before me. Unlike the preparation for my previous two books when I asked people in the 1990s to recall events from the 1970s, I would now ask people in the 21st century to recall events from the 1960s. Also, based on articles I had read, I was left with the impression that the Marvelettes had issues about how they were treated during their time at Motown. I was also undecided as to how I would handle "the Wanda situation." In my first conversation with Katherine, I asked her how Wanda was doing. Obviously, she was cautious about opening up to a complete stranger she was speaking with over the phone for the first time. Her response was, "Well, what have you heard?" Only what I read in Raynoma's book, *Berry and Me*, and also from Susan Whithall's *Women of Motown* book that she was too ill to grant interviews, I told her. In addition to confirming what I already knew, Katherine alerted me to a 1996 article in the *Globe* tabloid that gave a damning account of Wanda's condition as told from the perspective of someone in Inkster. Nevertheless, from the start, I debated internally over how much information I would reveal about Wanda's condition and lifestyle, and what happened during the 1960s and beyond that might have caused it. And this was assuming that either Katherine, or someone else close to the situation was willing to talk about it. As someone reminded me, "Keep in mind, Wanda is still alive, and she does have children." I knew I couldn't totally circumvent the issue simply because whenever I told anyone familiar with the Marvelettes, other than just as a passing interest, that I was writing a book about the group, their immediate response was, "Damn, what happened with Wanda?" Also, I was, and continue to be, a *huge* Wanda fan. This is a woman whose voice graced the lead of my favorite Marvelettes' songs and whose beauty speaks for itself.

It was roughly a year before Katherine opened up to me about Wanda's habits during the time the Marvelettes were in operation. And open up she did. I pointed out to Katherine the ol' "Wanda is still alive and she does have kids" issue. Her position was "Once the article in the *Globe* came out, everybody knew about Wanda. Besides, her kids know who she is." Frankly, it was a rude awakening, although I knew it was true. However, it busted a bubble in my eyes and I was forced to confront the truth behind the image of the entertainer who I'd only heard on vinyl, and seen in photos and on the limited video footage available. Katherine further stated, "Anybody in the inner circle could recognize that [Wanda] had a problem. For me to say something more about it would not be unheard of because the thing of it is, is that those in the industry expected it anyway." Fine. I can live with that. I am also at peace by having spoken to Wanda's sister, BeBe, who gave me her blessings and her support despite knowledge that this book would touch on Wanda's problems. Nevertheless, I tried to be tactful regarding what I chose to go public with; however, I am not naïve to think that there won't be any backlash or any, "Damn, did you read what Katherine had to say about Wanda?!" comments regarding the contents of this book from those who feel I should have left "the Wanda situation" alone and stuck to the music.

From the start, I found Katherine to be very honest and direct. I did not set out to write a positive story or a negative story, but the real story. In addition to "the Wanda situation," I knew there would be other issues I would have to confront: the Marvelettes not receiving a gold record for "Please Mr. Postman," how they were pushed aside after their initial success, not being invited to *Motown 25*, etc. ... On some occasions I knew I was opening old wounds with some of my questions to Katherine, yet it was important to her that the story of the Marvelettes be told as accurately as her memory would allow. As the composition of this book was winding down, she told me, "Anything I have said, you can put in there. Most people know I won't say anything I don't mean. There's no point in sugarcoating something that wasn't sugarcoated. If you tell the truth, who can go against you? The bottom line is that this is the truth as I remember it, and if somebody doesn't agree with it then *I* will address it." Despite some of her blunt comments, Katherine claims to hold no bitterness or regrets about her time as a professional singer and is quite thankful for the experience.

The story of the Marvelettes is not a pretty one. Again, of the five original members, one is deceased, one was overcome by the pressure of being in the industry at such a young age and dropped out, and one was victimized by the dark side of the entertainment industry. Also, one gets the impression that the group was snake-bitten. The Marvelettes' greatest professional triumphs came during

Motown's formative years. Thus, they were unable to fully capitalize on the Artist Development training that came several years later, or the advancements in the Civil Rights Movement that created avenues for black entertainers to appear on television in larger numbers.

I did not deliberately set out to write a negative diatribe against Motown Record Corporation, and I hope the end result is not anti-Motown. I, like millions of others, have received great joy from the music churned out by the numerous artists that recorded under the Motown banner. However, Motown was part of the entertainment industry, and the entertainment industry is a business. Berry Gordy, Jr., is to be revered for what he built Motown into, particularly at a time when starting up a black-owned record company was not exactly a thriving business. Nevertheless, the powers that be at Motown understandably chose not to grant any interviews for this book; understandably, because they knew in advance they would be confronted with such issues as pressuring the Marvelettes to drop out of high school during the run of "Please Mr. Postman," not receiving a gold record for the song, and why they weren't invited to *Motown 25*.

Throughout this journey, I have developed a greater admiration for the Marvelettes' songs, and also the Marvelettes as individuals. During the course of writing this book, I have also experienced numerous ups and downs. However, it has truly been a labor of love, and I am thankful and honored that God chose me as His vehicle to do this.

The Marvelettes Discography

SINGLES

(The Del-Rhythmetts with Gladys Horton)
"Chic-A-Boomer" / "I Need Your Love"
   (JVB Records 5000 1959)

Letters in parenthesis indicate who sang lead:
(G) Gladys Horton, (W) Wanda Young Rogers, (A) Ann Bogan

"Please Mr. Postman" (G) / "So Long Baby" (W)
   (US Tamla 54046, August 21, 1961; UK, Fontana 355,
   November 1961)

"Twistin' Postman" (G) / "I Want a Guy" (W)
   (US Tamla 54054, December 6, 1961; UK, Fontana 386,
   March 1962)

"Playboy" (G) / "All the Love I've Got" (G)
   (US Tamla 54060, April 9, 1962)

"Beechwood 4-5789" (G) / "Someday, Someway" (G)
   (US Tamla 54065, July 11, 1962; UK Oriole 1764,
   September 1962)

"Strange I Know" **(G)** / "Too Strong to Be Strung Along" **(G)**
(US Tamla 54072, October 29, 1962)

"Locking Up My Heart" **(G & W)** / "Forever" **(W)**
(US Tamla 54077, February 15, 1963; UK Oriole 1817, April 1963)

"My Daddy Knows Best" **(G)** / "Tie a String Around Your Finger" **(G)**
(US Tamla 54082, July 1, 1963)

"As Long As I Know He's Mine" **(G)** / "Little Girl Blue" **(G)**
(US Tamla 54088, October 14, 1963; UK Stateside 251, January 1964)

"Too Hurt to Cry, Too Much in Love to Say Goodbye" **(G)** / "Come on Home" **(G)**
(as the Darnells)
(US Gordy 7024, October 27, 1963)

"He's a Good Guy (Yes He Is)" **(G)** / "Goddess of Love" **(W)**
(US Tamla 54091, January 29, 1964; UK Stateside 273, March 1964)

"You're My Remedy" **(W)** / A Little Bit of Sympathy, A Little Bit of Love" **(G)**
(US Tamla 54097, June 8, 1964; UK Stateside 334, September 1964)

"Too Many Fish in the Sea" **(G)** / "A Need for Love" **(G)**
(US Tamla 5102, October 10, 1964; UK Stateside 369, January 1965)

"I'll Keep Holding On" **(W)** / "No Time for Tears" **(W)**
(US Tamla 54116, May 11, 1965; UK Tamla-Motown 518, June 1965)

"Danger Heartbreak Dead Ahead" **(W)** / "Your Cheating Ways" **(G)**

> (US Tamla 54120, July 23, 1965; UK Tamla-Motown 535, October 1965)

"Don't Mess with Bill" **(W)** / "Anything You Wanna Do" **(G)**

> (US Tamla 54126, November 26, 1965; UK Tamla-Motown 546, January 1966)

"You're the One" **(W)** / "Paper Boy" **(G)**

> (US Tamla 54131, April 4, 1966; UK Tamla-Motown 562, May 1966)

"The Hunter Gets Captured By the Game" **(W)** / "I Think I Can Change You" **(G)**

> (US Tamla 54143, December 27, 1966; UK Tamla-Motown 594, February 1967)

"When You're Young and in Love" **(W)** / "The Day You Take One [You Have to Take the Other]" **(W)**

> (US Tamla 54150, April 20, 1967; UK Tamla-Motown 609, May 1967; UK Tamla-Motown 939, February 1975)

"My Baby Must Be a Magician" **(W)** / "I Need Someone" **(G)**

> (US Tamla 54158, November 21, 1967; UK Tamla-Motown 639, January 1968)

"Here I Am Baby" **(W)** / "Keep Off, No Trespassing" **(G)**

> (US Tamla 54166, May 2, 1968; UK Tamla-Motown 659, June 1968)

"Destination: Anywhere" **(W)** / "What's Easy for Two Is Hard for One" **(W)**

> (US Tamla 54171, August 27, 1968)

"I'm Gonna Hold on As Long As I Can" **(A)** / "Don't Make Hurting Me a Habit" **(W)**

> (US Tamla 54177, December 23, 1968)

"Reachin' for Something I Can't Have" **(W)** / "Destination: Anywhere" **(W)**
>   (UK Tamla-Motown 701, June 1969)

"That's How Heartaches Are Made" **(W)** / "Rainy Mourning" **(W)**
>   (US Tamla 54186, September 23, 1969)

"Marionette" **(W)** / "After All" **(W)**
>   (US Tamla 54198, November 3, 1970)

"A Breath Taking Guy" **(W)** / "You're the One for Me Bobby" **(W)**
>   (US Tamla 54213, January 11, 1971)

"Reachin' for Something I Can't Have" **(W)** / "Here I Am Baby" **(W)**
>   (UK Tamla-Motown 860, September 1973)

"Finders Keepers, Losers Weepers" **(G)** / "Do Like I Do" **(Kim Weston)**
>   (UK Tamla-Motown 1000, August 1975)

"Holding on with Both Hands" **(G)** / ?
>   (UK Motorcity 16, 1989)

EPs

The Marvelettes
>   (UK Tamla-Motown 2003, March 1965)

Greatest Hits
>   (US Tamla 60253, 1967)

The Marvelettes
>   (US Tamla 60274, 1967 different from UK issue)

ALBUMS

Please Mr. Postman
(US Tamla LP 228, November 20, 1961; UK Motown LP 5266ML,
  September 1982)

  "Angel"
  "I Want a Guy"
  "Please Mr. Postman"
  "So Long Baby"
  "I Know How It Feels"
  "Way Over There"
  "Happy Days"
  "You Don't Want Me No More"
  "All the Love I've Got"
  "Whisper"
  "I Apologize"

The Marvelettes Sing (*Smash Hits of 1962*)
(US Tamla LP 229, April 1962)

  "Mashed Potato Time"
  "Love Letters"
  "The One Who Really Loves You"
  "Twistin' the Night Away"
  "Hey Baby"
  "Twistin' Postman"
  "Good Luck Charm"
  "Slow Twist" (duet with Mickey Stevenson)
  "Lover Please"
  "Dream Baby"

Playboy
(US Tamla LP 231, July 1962)

  "Playboy"
  "Mix It Up"
  "Beechwood 4-5789"

"I'm Hooked"
"I Think I Can Change You"
"Forever"
"Someday, Someway"
"Goddess of Love"
"You Should Know"
"I've Got to (Cry Over You)"

The Marvelous Marvelettes
(US Tamla LP 237, February 28, 1963; US Motown CD
  31453-0365-2, 1994)
(UK Tamla-Motown LP 11008, April 1965—different from
  US issue)

"Strange I Know"
"I Forgot About You"
"Locking Up My Heart"
"Which Way Did He Go"
"Silly Boy"
"It's Gonna Take a Lot of Doing"
"Smart Aleck"
"My Daddy Knows Best"
"Too Strong to Be Strung Along"
"Why Must You Go"

The Marvelettes on Stage, Recorded Live
(US Tamla LP 243, July 1963)

"Beechwood 4-5789"
"Strange I Know"
"Someday, Someway"
"Locking Up My Heart"
"Twistin' Postman"
"Tossing and Turning"
"So Long Baby"
"Playboy"

The Marvelettes Greatest Hits
(US Tamla LP 253, February 16, 1966; US Motown LP M5-180,
  June 1981)

   "Don't Mess with Bill"
   "You're My Remedy"
   "Locking Up My Heart"
   "As Long As I Know He's Mine"
   "Too Many Fish in the Sea"
   "Danger, Heartbreak Dead Ahead"
   "Please Mr. Postman"
   "Playboy"
   "Strange I Know"
   "Forever"
   "Twistin' Postman"
   "Beechwood 4-5789"

The Marvelettes
(US Tamla LP 274, March 6, 1967; UK Tamla-Motown LP 11052,
  June 1967)

   "Barefootin' "
   "Message to Michael"
   "The Hunter Gets Captured By the Game"
   "When You're Young and in Love"
   "I Know Better"
   "I Can't Turn Around"
   "He Was Really Sayin' Somethin' "
   "The Day You Take One [You Have to Take the Other]"
   "When I Need You"
   "Keep Off, No Trespassing"
   "The Night Was Made for Love"
   "I Need Someone"

Sophisticated Soul
(US Tamla LP 286, August 26, 1968; UK Tamla-Motown 11090,
    January 1969)

"My Baby Must Be a Magician"
"Destination: Anywhere"
"I'm Gonna Hold on As Long As I Can"
"Here I Am Baby"
"You're the One for Me Bobby"
"Reachin' for Something I Can't Have"
"Your Love Can Save Me"
"You're the One"
"Don't Make Hurting Me a Habit"
"What's Easy for Two Is Hard for One"
"The Stranger"
"Someway, Somehow"

In Full Bloom
(US Tamla LP 288, September 16, 1969; UK Tamla-Motown 11145,
    May 1970)

"Seeing Is Believing"
"Sunshine Days"
"That's How Heartaches Are Made"
"The Truth's Outside My Door"
"I Have Someone (Who Loves Me Too)"
"Uptown"
"At Last I See Love As It Really Is"
"Now Is the Time for Love"
"Too Many Tears, Too Many Times"
"Rainy Mourning"
"Everybody Knows (But You)"
"Love Silent, Love Deep"

The Return of the Marvelettes
(US Tamla LP 305, September 15, 1970; UK Tamla-Motown 11177,
  not issued)

> "So I Can Love You"
> "Marionette"
> "That's How Heartaches Are Made"
> "A Breath Taking Guy"
> "No More Tearstained Makeup"
> "Uptown"
> "Someday We'll Be Together"
> "After All"
> "Our Lips Just Seem to Rhyme Every Time"
> "Fading Away"
> "Take Me Where You Go"
> "I'll Be in Trouble"

Anthology
(Motown M7-875, May 15, 1975)

> "Please Mr. Postman"
> "So Long Baby"
> "Twistin' Postman"
> "Playboy"
> "Beechwood 4-5789"
> "Someday, Someway"
> "Strange I Know"
> "Locking Up My Heart"
> "Forever"
> "My Daddy Knows Best"
> "As Long As I Know He's Mine"
> "He's a Good Guy (Yes He Is)"
> "You're My Remedy"
> "Too Many Fish in the Sea"

"I'll Keep Holding On"
"Danger Heartbreak Dead Ahead"
"Don't Mess with Bill"
"You're the One"
"The Hunter Gets Captured By the Game"
"When You're Young and in Love"
"The Day You Take One [You Have to Take the Other]"
"My Baby Must Be a Magician"
"Here I Am Baby"
"Destination: Anywhere"
"I'm Gonna Hold on As Long As I Can"
"That's How Heartaches Are Made"
"Marionette"
"A Breath Taking Guy"

The Marvelettes: Compact Command Performances
(US Motown CD 6169, February 1986; US Motown CD 9056,
  June 1987; UK Tamla-Motown 72446, March 1987)

"Please Mr. Postman"
"Twistin' Postman"
"Playboy"
"Beechwood 4-5789"
"Someday, Someway"
"Strange I Know"
"Locking Up My Heart"
"Forever"
"My Daddy Knows Best"
"As Long As I Know He's Mine"
"He's a Good Guy (Yes He Is)"
"You're My Remedy"
"Too Many Fish in the Sea"
"I'll Keep Holding On"
"Danger Heartbreak Dead Ahead"

"Don't Mess with Bill"
"You're the One"
"The Hunter Gets Captured By the Game"
"When You're Young and in Love"
"The Day You Take One [You Have to Take the Other]"
"My Baby Must Be a Magician"
"Here I Am Baby"
"Destination: Anywhere"

The Marvelettes + Sophisticated Soul
(US Motown CD 8055T, January 1987)
"Barefootin' "
"Message to Michael"
"The Hunter Gets Captured By the Game"
"When You're Young and in Love"
"I Know Better"
"I Can't Turn Around"
"He Was Really Sayin' Somethin' "
"The Day You Take One [You Have to Take the Other]"
"When I Need You"
"Keep Off, No Trespassing"
"The Night Was Made for Love"
"I Need Someone"
"My Baby Must Be a Magician"
"Destination: Anywhere"
"I'm Gonna Hold on As Long As I Can"
"Here I Am Baby"
"You're the One for Me Bobby"
"Reachin' for Something I Can't Have"
"Your Love Can Save Me"
"You're the One"
"Don't Make Hurting Me a Habit"
"What's Easy for Two Is Hard for One"
"The Stranger"
"Someway, Somehow"

The Marvelettes Now!
(UK Motorcity 38, 1990)

"Don't Mess with Bill"
"Secret Love Affair"
"Just in the Nick of Time"
"My Baby Must Be a Magician"
"You Bring the Love into My Life"
"Too Many Fish in the Sea"
"Holding on with Both Hands"
"Beechwood 4-5789"
"Used to Be a Playboy"
"When You're Young and in Love"

Deliver: The Singles 1961–1971
(US Tamla 2-CD 37463-6259-2, 1993)

"Please Mr. Postman"
"So Long Baby"
"Twistin' Postman"
"I Want a Guy"
"Playboy"
"Beechwood 4-5789"
"Someday, Someway"
"Strange I Know"
"Locking Up My Heart"
"Forever"
"My Daddy Knows Best"
"Tie a String Around Your Finger"
"As Long As I Know He's Mine"
"Little Girl Blue"
"Too Hurt to Cry, Too Much in Love to Say Goodbye"
"He's a Good Guy (Yes He Is)"
"Finders Keepers, Losers Weepers"
"You're My Remedy"
"A Little Bit of Sympathy, A Little Bit of Love"

"Too Many Fish in the Sea"
"A Need for Love"
"I'll Keep Holding On"
"No Time for Tears"
"Danger Heartbreak Dead Ahead"
"Your Cheating Ways"
"Don't Mess with Bill"
"Anything You Wanna Do"
"You're the One"
"Paper Boy"
"The Hunter Gets Captured By the Game"
"When You're Young and in Love"
"The Day You Take One [You Have to Take the Other]"
"My Baby Must Be a Magician"
"Here I Am Baby"
"Reachin' for Something I Can't Have"
"Destination: Anywhere"
"What's Easy for Two Is Hard for One"
"I'm Gonna Hold on As Long As I Can"
"That's How Heartaches Are Made"
"Rainy Mourning"
"Marionette"
"A Breath Taking Guy"

The Best of the Marvelettes
(US Motown Milestones CD 31453-0408-2, July 25, 1995;
 UK Motown Milestones 530408-2, 1996)

"Please Mr. Postman"
"Twistin' Postman"
"Playboy"
"Beechwood 4-5789"
"Strange I Know"
"Locking Up My Heart"

"You're My Remedy"
"Too Many Fish in the Sea"
"I'll Keep Holding On"
"Danger Heartbreak Dead Ahead"
"Don't Mess with Bill"
"You're the One"
"The Hunter Gets Captured By the Game"
"When You're Young and in Love"
"The Day You Take One [You Have to Take the Other]"
"My Baby Must Be a Magician"
"Here I Am Baby"
"Destination: Anywhere"
"That's How Heartaches Are Made"
"Marionette"

The Ultimate Collection
(Motown CD 530856, 1998)

"Please Mr. Postman"
"Playboy"
"So Long Baby"
"Beechwood 4-5789"
"Someday, Someway"
"Strange I Know"
"Too Strong to Be Strong Along"
"Twistin' Postman"
"Locking Up My Heart"
"Forever"
"My Daddy Knows Best"
"As Long As I Know He's Mine"
"He's a Good Guy (Yes He Is)"
"You're My Remedy"
"Too Many Fish in the Sea"
"I'll Keep Holding On"

"Danger Heartbreak Dead Ahead"
"Don't Mess with Bill"
"You're The One"
"My Baby Must Be a Magician"
"The Hunter Gets Captured By the Game"
"Destination: Anywhere"
"Here I Am Baby"
"When You're Young and in Love"
"That's How Heartaches Are Made"

The Essential Collection
(Spectrum CD 5548592, 1999)
"I Just Can't Let Him Down"
"On the Other Side of Town"
"Maybe I Dried My Tears for the Last Time"
"Because I Love Him"
"When I Need You"
"Reachin' for Something I Can't Have"
"When You're Young and in Love"
"Our Lips Just Seem to Rhyme Every Time"
"Caught You Puttin' the Game on Love"
"I Have Someone (Who Loves Me Too)"
"I Need Someone"
"Danger Heartbreak Dead Ahead"
"Please Mr. Postman"
"Sugar's Never Been as Sweet As You"
"The Boy from Crosstown"
"Your Cheating Ways"
"Too Hurt to Cry, Too Much in Love to Say Goodbye"
"Finders Keepers, Losers Weepers"

20th Century Masters—The Millennium
(Motown CD 159407, 2000)

"Please Mr. Postman"
"Playboy"
"Beechwood 4-5789"
"Locking Up My Heart"
"Too Many Fish in the Sea"
"I'll Keep Holding On"
"Danger Heartbreak Dead Ahead"
"Don't Mess with Bill"
"The Hunter Gets Captured By the Game"
"When You're Young and in Love"
"My Baby Must Be a Magician"

THE CHARTS

(Billboard)

Title	Debut Date (Pop)	Peak Position
Please Mr. Postman	9/4/61	1 (1 week)
Twistin' Postman	1/27/62	34
Playboy	5/2/62	7
Beechwood 4-5789	8/11/62	17
Someday, Someway		
Strange I Know	12/1/62	49
Locking Up My Heart	3/23/63	44
Forever	5/4/63	78
My Daddy Knows Best	8/3/63	67
As Long As I Know He's Mine	11/9/63	47
He's A Good Guy (Yes He Is)	2/22/64	55
You're My Remedy	7/4/64	48
Too Many Fish In the Sea	11/7/64	25
I'll Keep Holding On	5/29/65	34
Danger Heartbreak Dead Ahead	8/14/65	61
Don't Mess with Bill	1/1/66	7
You're the One	4/23/66	48
The Hunter Gets Captured By the Game	1/21/67	13
When You're Young and In Love	4/22/67	23
My Baby Must Be a Magician	12/16/67	17
Here I Am Baby	6/8/68	44
Destination: Anywhere	10/5/68	63
I'm Gonna Hold On As Long As I Can	1/1/69	76
That's How Heartaches Are Made	11/8/69	97

(Billboard)

Title	Debut Date (R&B)	Peak Position
Please Mr. Postman	9/11/61	1 (7 weeks)
Twistin' Postman	2/17/62	13
Playboy	5/26/62	4
Beechwood 4-5789	8/18/62	7
Someday, Someway	9/15/62	8
Strange I Know	12/29/62	10
Locking Up My Heart	5/4/63	25
Forever	6/15/63	24
My Daddy Knows Best		
As Long As I Know He's Mine	N/A	
He's A Good Guy (Yes He Is)	N/A	
You're My Remedy	N/A	
Too Many Fish In the Sea	1/30/65	15
I'll Keep Holding On	6/19/65	11
Danger Heartbreak Dead Ahead	9/11/65	11
Don't Mess with Bill	1/15/66	3
You're the One	5/21/66	20
The Hunter Gets Captured By the Game	2/4/67	2 (3 weeks)
When You're Young and In Love	5/13/67	9
My Baby Must Be a Magician	12/30/67	8
Here I Am Baby	6/22/68	14
Destination: Anywhere	10/12/68	28
I'm Gonna Hold On As Long As I Can		
That's How Heartaches Are Made		

(Cash Box)

Title	Debut Date (Pop)	Peak Position
Please Mr. Postman	9/16/61	2
Twistin' Postman	1/27/62	32
Playboy	5/5/62	8
Beechwood 4-5789	8/4/62	18
Someday, Someway		
Strange I Know	12/1/62	50
Locking Up My Heart	3/16/62	54
Forever	5/25/63	89
My Daddy Knows Best	7/27/63	89
As Long As I Know He's Mine	11/9/63	43
He's A Good Guy (Yes He Is)	2/22/64	59
You're My Remedy	7/4/64	54
Too Many Fish In the Sea	11/14/64	21
I'll Keep Holding On	6/5/65	36
Danger Heartbreak Dead Ahead	8/14/65	57
Don't Mess with Bill	1/1/66	9
You're the One	4/23/66	46
The Hunter Gets Captured By the Game	1/28/67	16
When You're Young and In Love	4/29/67	30
My Baby Must Be a Magician	12/16/67	10
Here I Am Baby	5/25/68	44
Destination: Anywhere	10/5/68	58
I'm Gonna Hold On As Long As I Can	1/25/69	49
That's How Heartaches Are Made	11/15/69	81

(Cash Box)

Title	Debut Date (Black Contemporary)	Peak Position
Please Mr. Postman	9/30/61	1 (6 weeks)
Twistin' Postman	1/27/62	14
Playboy	5/5/62	2 (1 week)
Beechwood 4-5789	8/4/62	6
Someday, Someway	9/22/62	50
Strange I Know	11/24/62	27
Locking Up My Heart	3/9/63	17
Forever	5/25/63	33
My Daddy Knows Best	7/27/63	43
As Long As I Know He's Mine	11/9/63	3
He's A Good Guy (Yes He Is)	2/22/64	18
You're My Remedy	7/4/64	16
Too Many Fish In the Sea	11/14/64	5
I'll Keep Holding On	5/29/65	18
Danger Heartbreak Dead Ahead	8/14/65	18
Don't Mess with Bill	1/1/66	3
You're the One	4/23/66	17
The Hunter Gets Captured By the Game	1/21/67	1 (1 week)
When You're Young and In Love	4/29/67	10
My Baby Must Be a Magician	12/16/67	3
Here I Am Baby	5/25/68	27
Destination: Anywhere	9/7/68	14
I'm Gonna Hold On As Long As I Can		
That's How Heartaches Are Made		

Bibliography

Betrock, Alan. *Girl Groups: The Story of a Sound.* New York: Delilah Books, 1982.

Brasler, Wayne. "The Marvelettes: Motown's First Ladies." *Goldmine* 8 June 1984 pp. 34+.

Bronson, Fred. *The Billboard Book of Number One Hits.* New York: Billboard Publications, Inc., 1988.

Bronson, Fred. Liner notes, *The Marvelettes—Deliver: The Singles 1961–1971.* Motown 37463-6259-2, 1993.

Clemente, John. *Girl Groups: Fabulous Females That Rocked the World.* Iola, WI: Krause, Pubs., 2000.

Dahl, Bill. *Motown: The Golden Years.* Iola, WI: Krause, Pubs., 2001.

Dahl, Bill. "Smokey Robinson and the Miracles: Ooh Baby Baby." *Goldmine* 10 December 1993 pp. 14–34.

Douglas, Tony. *Lonely Teardrops: The Jackie Wilson Story.* London: Sanctuary Publishing, Ltd., 1997.

Downey, Pat, Albert, George, and Hoffman, Frank. *Cash Box Pop Singles Charts.* Englewood, CO: Libraries, Ltd., 1994

Gaar, Gillian G. *She's a Rebel: The History of Women in Rock & Roll.* Seattle, WA: Seal Press, 1992.

George, Nelson. *Where Did Our Love Go? The Rise and Fall of the Motown Sound.* London: St. Martin's Press, 1985.

Gordy, Berry. *To Be Loved: The Music, the Magic, the Memories of Motown.* New York: Warner Books, Inc., 1994.

Gordy Singleton, Raynoma with Brown, Bryan and Eichler, Mim. *Berry, Me, and Motown: The Untold Story*. Chicago: Contemporary Books, Inc., 1990.

Greig, Charlene. *Will You Still Love Me Tomorrow? Girl Groups from the 50s On*. London: Virago Press, Ltd., 1989.

Griffin, Rita. "Rites for Ex-Motown Singer." *Michigan Chronicle* 19 January 1980 p. A 01 1.

"Original Marvelette Dies of Sickle Cell Anemia at 35," *Jet* 7 February 1980 p. 60.

Posner, Gerald. *Motown: Music, Money, Sex, and Power*. New York: Random House, 2002.

Reeves, Martha and Bego, Mark. *Dancing in the Street: Confessions of a Motown Diva*. New York: Hyperion, 1994.

Robinson, William "Smokey" and David Ritz. *Smokey: Inside My Life*, New York: McGraw-Hill Publishing Co., 1989.

Smith, Suzanne E. *Dancing in the Street: Motown and the Culture Politics of Detroit*. Cambridge, MA: Harvard University Press, 1999.

Taraborrelli, J. Randy. *Call Her Miss Ross*. New York: Birch Lane Press, 1989.

Taraborrelli, J. Randy. *Motown: Hot Wax, City Cool & Solid Gold*. Garden City, New York: Dolphin, 1986.

Turner, Steve, *Trouble Man: The Life and Death of Marvin Gaye*, Ecco, New York, 2000.

Whitaker, Charles. "Living with Lupus." *Ebony* July 2001 pp. 54–57.

Whitall, Susan, *Women of Motown: An Oral History*. New York: Avon Books, 1998.

Whitburn, Joel, Billboard *Top 10 Singles Charts 1955–2000*. Menomonee Falls, WI: Record Research, Inc., 2001.

Whitburn, Joel, *Top R&B Singles 1945–1995*. Menomonee Falls, WI: Record Research, Inc., 1996.

Wilson, Mary. *Dreamgirl: My Life As a Supreme*. New York: St. Martin's Press, 1986.

Index

A Touch of Classic Soul: Soul Singers of the Early 1970s

Read about 35 of soul music's biggest stars of the early 1970s. Features interviews and profiles on the Dells, the Intruders, the Manhattans, the Whispers, the Spinners, Gladys Knight and the Pips, Bobby Womack, Freda Payne, the Dramatics, the O'Jays, Al Green, Isaac Hayes, Barry White, Bloodstone, Blue Magic, Chairmen of the Board, Millie Jackson, the Chi-Lites, the Delfonics, the Friends of Distinction, the Emotions, First Choice, the Three Degrees, Jean Knight, War, the Main Ingredient, the Temprees, Harold Melvin and the Blue Notes, the Staple Singers, the Moments, New Birth, the Ohio Players, Billy Paul, the Stylistics, and Betty Wright.

A Touch of Classic Soul 2: The Late 1970s

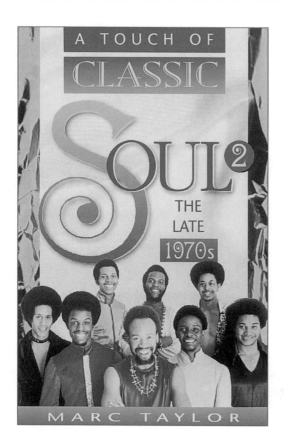

Read about 31 of soul music's biggest stars of the mid to late-1970s. Features interviews and profiles on George Benson, Parliament/Funkadelic, the Brothers Johnson, Earth, Wind and Fire, Deniece Williams, Candi Staton, Peaches and Herb, the Sylvers, the Persuaders, the Isley Brothers, Rufus featuring Chaka Khan, Evelyn "Champagne" King, Con Funk Shun, Sister Sledge, Enchantment, Chic, the Commodores, Donna Summer, Natalie Cole, B. T Express, A Taste of Honey, GQ, Brass Construction, the Trammps, L.T.D., Rose Royce, the Joneses, Soul Generation, Black Ivory, the Escorts, and Heat-wave.

About the Author

Marc Taylor has been writing
about soul music for more
than a decade. The author of
*A Touch of Classic Soul: Soul
Singers of the Early 1970s* and
*A Touch of Classic Soul 2:
The Late 1970s,* he has written
for numerous publications,
including *Goldmine.* He lives
in New York.

Order Form

_____ *A Touch of Classic Soul: Soul Singers of the Early 1970s*

_____ *A Touch of Classic Soul 2: The Late 1970s*

$18 for one book;
$30 if ordering both books.
Includes all applicable taxes and postage.

Aloiv Publishing Company
P.O. Box 34-0484
Jamaica, NY 11434
Telephone: (212) 712-8745
Fax: (718) 528-9778

Name_____

Address _____

Address _____

City _____

State _____ Zip_____- _____